Rabbi Scott Hausman-Weiss

ANIMALS
IN JEWISH
THOUGHT AND
TRADITION

ANIMALS IN JEWISH THOUGHT AND TRADITION

Ronald H. Isaacs

JASON ARONSON INC.
Northvale, New Jersey
Jerusalem

This book was set in 12 pt. Corona by Alabama Book Composition of Deatsville, Alabama.

Library of Congress Cataloging-in-Publication Data

Isaacs, Ronald H.
    Animals in Jewish thought and tradition / by Ronald H. Isaacs.
       p.   cm.
    Includes bibliographical references and index.
    ISBN 0-7657-9976-6 (alk. paper)
    1. Animals in the Bible. 2. Bible. O.T.—Criticism,
interpretation, etc. 3. Animals in rabbinical literature.
4. Animals—Religious aspects—Judaism. I. Title.
BS663.I83 2000
296.3′693—dc21   97–19293

Manufactured in the United States of America. For information and catalog write to Jason Aronson Inc., 230 Livingston Street, Northvale, New Jersey 07647, or visit our website: www.aronson.com

For Fallon, Zoë, and
Drs. Stephen and Charles Schwirck

Contents

Introduction

Introduction

References to the animal kingdom pervade biblical, Talmudic, and midrashic writings. Scores of animal species, including domestic and wild mammals, insects, fish, and birds appear throughout these texts. Many metaphorical and allegorical allusions to animals are also found in different literary forms among Jewish writings. In talmudic and legendary literature alone, there are thirty-six Hebrew and Aramaic animal tales designated as *fox fables*. There is even a conception that each species of animal sings its own particular hymn of glory to its Creator, and the ancient compilation known as *Perek Shirah* ('Chapter of the Song') lists the particular scriptural verses used by God's creatures in praise of Him. There are also a variety of animal tales in literature of the Middle Ages, as well as in that of the modern period. All of the literature related to the animal world can provide the reader with a fascinating new understanding of the role that the animals play in Jewish tradition.

There is also an extensive Jewish literature related to the treatment and proper care of animals. In the fourth commandment of the Ten Commandments God commands not only humans to rest, but animals as well! It seems that wherever we turn, Jewish tradition regards the life of all of God's creatures—animals included—as sacred.

Philosophers, too, throughout the centuries have raised a variety of interesting questions concerning the animal kingdom, including the questions of why God created animals in the first place; whether animals, like humans, have souls; and whether animals go to Heaven.

This volume introduces readers to the fascinating world and role of the animal kingdom as seen throughout Jewish history. Material is drawn from a variety of traditional sources, including the Bible, the Talmud, the midrash, various philosophical works, and short stories.

I hope that this book will bring you to a closer understanding of the role that animals play in Jewish law, custom, and tradition.

RONALD H. ISAACS

An Introduction to Animals of the Bible and the Talmud

There are some 120 names of animals in the Bible, representing mammals, birds, and reptiles in particular. According to the *Encyclopedia Judaica* (Vol. 3), of the 86 mammals, 359 birds, and 76 species of reptiles in Israel, about 37, 38, and 12 respectively are specified by name in the Bible.

Many of the references to the animals have become controversial because some animals have more than one name in Hebrew. In addition, some Hebrew words can mean more than one animal. There is a scarcity of animal names in talmudic literature because Jewish law mentions them in the main only for the Jewish dietary laws and laws of slaughtering.

The Bible uses two main terms to denote a mammal. The usual one is *behemah*, which refers to both domestic and wild mammals, with seven species of the latter included among the mammals permissible as food (Deut. 14:5). The other is *chaya*, which is a term that can mean either a domestic or wild animal. For instance, in Leviticus 11:2, the Bible uses *chaya* to refer to domesticated animals with split hooves and who chew their cud. However, another passage speaks of hunting any beast (*chaya*) where the word refers to a wild animal (Lev. 17:13).

In talmudic literature, *chaya*, a wild mammal, and *behemah*, a domestic mammal, are clearly distinguished from each other, with differing laws applying to each.

Except possibly for Solomon, who took enough scientific interest in animals to classify them loosely (as beasts, fowl, creeping things, and fish) and to lecture on them (1 Kings 4:33–34), the ancient Israelites were not particularly inquisitive when it came to wild animals. Rather, they took a very practical attitude, judging animals according to how beneficial or damaging they were to people. Wild animals were not permitted to be used in sacrifices because they did not represent wealth, and killing them would therefore not be a true loss. As a result, to the ancient Israelites, most wild animals were not of much use.

Nine animals in the Bible are referred to as permitted for food, namely the deer, gazelle, and fallow deer; the addax, bison, and oryx; the wild goat; the wild ox; and the ibex. In early times the wild ox had disappeared. The rest of these animals were found in Israel and neighboring countries until the end of the nineteenth century. The primary reason for their disappearance was that they were hunted for meat and had excellent skins that could be used or sold for substantial profit. This has also led to the elimination of the larger carnivorous animals such as the lion and the bear.

In Crusader times the lion was still to be found in Israel's south, the Negev. The hippopotamus disappeared many centuries ago, while ostriches and wild asses became extinct within the last century. Some species of leopards as well as the cheetah still exist in southern Israel.

Most domestic animals were domesticated as early as during the pre-biblical period. Engravings of camels and cattle have been found on rocks in Jordan, and clay images of goats, sheep, and pigs have been uncovered in the ancient city of Jericho dating from the fifth century B.C.E.

The Bible does not make mention of pets such as cats or dogs. Several breeds of dogs have appeared in ancient drawings uncovered in Israel. The mule and donkey were used in Israel much more than the horse. The raising of fowl can be attested to by a seal dating from the period of the Israelite kingdom and on which a cock is engraved.

Among the most frequently mentioned animals used in biblical parables and allegories as symbols of strength, cruelty, or dexterity are the lion, the leopard, the bear, the wolf, and the wild ox. For instance, the Book of Numbers 24:8–9 says of the Israelites, "God . . . is for them like the horns of the wild ox; they shall devour enemy nations, crush their bones . . . they crouch, they lie down like the lion; like the king of beasts."

The following are brief descriptions of a cross section of animals likely to have existed in biblical times:

Ass: Two Hebrew words were used for this animal—*atone* and *chamor*. In biblical times the ass served as both a form of transportation and a beast of burden. The ass was thought to have been domesticated in Neolithic times in Northeast Africa. The first biblical mention is during Abram's stay in Egypt (Gen. 12:16), but he had likely used asses as transport from Mesopotamia, where several breeds were said to have existed.

The ass is mentioned in one of the biblical injunctions regarding the care of animals. We learn that asses were not to be exploited in the

Book of Deuteronomy (22:10): "You shall not plow with an ox and an ass together."

Two significant biblical stories are noteworthy for the appearance of the ass. One is the speaking ass on which Balaam, prophet of the King of Moab, rode, recorded in the Book of Numbers 22. Ironically, this ass was not only able to speak, but was able to see the angel of the Lord. The Mishnah in Pirkei Avot (5:9) asserts that "the mouth of the ass was one of ten miracles that God created before the Sabbath."

A second story is found in the Book of Zechariah (9:9): "Behold your king comes to you, he is triumphant and victorious, lowly and riding upon an ass." Commenting on this verse, Bible scholars project that the reference here is to none other than the Messiah himself. Thus the ass becomes an animal that bears a rider whose mission is to bring peace and tranquility to a troubled world.

Bear: The Hebrew word for bear is *dov.* The gray-colored Syrian bear that once inhabited Israel became extinct in the early Twentieth Century because of pleasure hunting. In biblical times it was most likely to inhabit forests and deserts. The bear was extremely feared due to its ferocity and unpredictability. In fact, Amos's remark (5:19), "as if a man did flee from a lion and a bear did meet him" seems to be the Bible's equivalent of "out of the frying pan, into the fire."

Although the Bible (Lam. 3:10) speaks of a bear "lying in wait," two she-bears came boldly out of the woods to maul forty-two children who had taunted Elisha (2 Kings 2:24), and bears are also said to have been ranging and dangerous (Prov. 28:15). Apparently they were troublesome to shepherds, because David killed one that chased after his sheep.

Biblical authors had a fairly good knowledge of the bear and its behavior, and would often use it in their writings. Daniel (7:5) describes the bear as a frightening beast, while Isaiah (59:11) was impressed by the bear's roar and also described a cow and a bear feeding together, a symbolic image of Messianic times. Especially feared was a sow robbed of her cubs (2 Sam. 17:18).

Boar: In Hebrew, *chazeer meeya'ar*, a forest dweller, the wild boar is probably the ancestor of the modern pig. In the Bible, boars (because of their long and dangerous tusks) are mentioned solely as a menace—"the wild boar out of the wood does waste the vine" (Ps. 80:13). Excavated caves on Mount Carmel have shown that the boar was eaten in biblical times and that tools were fashioned from their tusks.

Camel: (In Hebrew, *Gamal.*) There has been much argument about the use of camels by the Patriarchs, but archaeology has shown that there were domesticated camels in Egypt at least 1,200 years earlier. The camel was useful in biblical times for both transportation and as a beast of burden. In the narrative from Genesis 24:35 onward camels formed an important part of the wealth of ancient Middle-Eastern countries, and were also used for long-distance travel. King David appointed an Ishmaelite as his camel master (1 Chron. 27:30), and the Queen of Sheba's baggage was carried on camels from Arabia.

Perhaps one of the most famous stories involving a camel relates to the finding of a suitable wife for Isaac by Eliezer, servant of Abraham:

"Let it come to pass, that the damsel to whom I shall say: Let down thy pitcher I pray you, that I may drink; and she shall say: Drink, and I will give your camels drink also; let the same be she that You have appointed for Your servant, even for Isaac" (Gen. 24:14).

Kindness to animals, in this case the camel, becomes the litmus test for the successful search, resulting in Rebekah being chosen as Isaac's wife!

Cat: Israel has a wild cat that lives in wooden

ravines in the north. A slightly larger jungle cat frequents fishponds and the Jordan River, but the Bible makes no mention of any of these.

This omission may have something to do with the fact that the cat was highly esteemed and venerated among Israel's enemies. Only in the Apocrypha are cats mentioned briefly, and identified with idolatry. In Jeremy's epistle (Bar. 6:22) to captives being taken to Babylon, where he warns them not to be frightened by pagan practices, he explains that in the foreign temples they can expect to see the faces of the idols blackened with smoke, and sitting on the images will be bats, swallows, and cats.

In Chad Gadya, the popular allegorical Passover hymn sung at the end of the Seder, the cat (*shunra* in Aramaic) is the first animal that is mentioned: "Then came the cat that ate the kid." Some commentators have suggested that the kid is symbolic of Joseph, who was sold into slavery at age 17 (the numerical value in *gematriah* of kid, *gedi*, is 17). By nature the cat is envious. Joseph's brothers, represented by the cat, were envious of Joseph and sold him to the Ishmaelites.

Deer: In biblical times, there were many different varieties of deer. Roe deer, sometimes called Carmel deer, survived into the Twentieth Century on Mount Carmel and Huleh

Lane. Red deer, sometimes called Solomon's deer, became extinct during the Crusades. All ruminants that had cloven hooves and chewed cud were permissible to be eaten, and Isaac was said to have been especially fond of venison. Because of their generally gentle nature (Prov. 5:19), it is possible that deer were tamed and kept for food by others besides King Solomon (1 Kings 4:23).

Deer were so well regarded that to compare the tribe of Naphtali to them was a compliment (Gen. 49:21). Their fleetness was noted by Isaiah (35:6) in a graphic image of a lame man leaping like a hart, and the deer is referred to in other biblical passages regarding speed, such as "my feet like hinds' feet" (2 Sam. 22:34).

Elephant: Although paleontologists have found bones and tusks of prehistoric elephants in the Jordan Valley and in other places in Israel, these animals were extinct in biblical times. There are twelve references to ivory in the Bible.

In the Apocrypha, the Books of Maccabees (1 Macc. 6:30, 35) have several references to the fighting elephants used against the Jews by the Seleucid, Antioches Epiphanes. In another story, Eleazar the Maccabean, who noticed that one elephant's canopy was higher than any other, concluded that this animal must bear the king. During the battle he managed to dodge all the attendant cavalry and foot soldiers to reach this elephant, creep under it, and kill it. As it died, the elephant sank down upon Eleazar, crushing him to death (Macc. 1:71; 6:34–37).

Fox: (In Hebrew, *shu'al.*) Israel has several species of foxes, including the red fox, which spends a great deal of time stalking small animals. The earliest references to foxes in the Bible are found in Judges 15:4, where we are told that Samson the Judge took 300 foxes, tied them by their tails, placed a firebrand between each, and let them loose in the Philistine cornfields. Some commentators suggest that the Bible refers here to jackals and not foxes.

Foxes were a nuisance to vineyards, which they invaded from the time the grapes began to ripen in the summer: "Take us the foxes, the little foxes that spoil our grapes, for our vines have tender grapes (Song of Songs 2:15). When Isaiah (5:2) describes someone planting a vineyard he notes that the farmer "built a tower in the midst of it." Guards were posted in these towers until the grapes were harvested in the fall.

Gazelle: (In Hebrew, *tzvee.*) Symbol of love and gracefulness, this swift and beautiful creature is still beloved in Israel. One of the ancient names of Israel was *Eretz Hatzvi*, meaning land of the gazelle. The gazelle's curiosity makes it bound away and then stop to look back, so that the Song of Songs (2:9) uses it as a comparison for a lover hiding behind a wall and peering from behind a lattice. Because the gazelle is gentle, Proverbs (5:19) urges wives to be "as the loving hind and pleasant roe."

Many other references to the gazelle relate to its swiftness. King David's mighty men were said to be as "swift as the roes upon the mountains" (1 Chron. 12:8), and Asahel could run so fast he was considered "as light of foot as a wild roe" (2 Sam. 12:18).

Goat: The goat was very useful to the Patriarchs (Gen. 15:9), for though it was kept with sheep it had the advantage of being able to thrive on poorer ground. The story of the twin brothers Jacob and Esau (Gen. 27:9) stresses the goat's value as meat, but normally only kids were used for food.

The goat was a key element in a sacrificial ritual that took place during the time of the Great Temple. The rite was derived from Leviticus (16:7): "And he shall take the two goats and set them before God at the door of the tent of meeting. And Aaron shall cast lots upon the two gates: one for God, and the other for Azazel." This ritual has given rise to the word scapegoat (i.e., the goat that escapes into the wilderness).

Ibex: Ancient Israel probably had more than one species of wild goat, but the only one to survive today is the ibex. These animals are still found from the north shore of the Dead Sea along the ridges bordering the shore to Eilat. The Ein Gedi preserve (note: *Ein Gedi*, means 'spring of the goat') is where David hid from Saul "upon the rocks of the wild goats" (1 Sam. 24:1–2). This has been a favorite hideaway for both goats and people since ancient times.

In discussing God's wisdom, Job (39:1) remarked on the secretiveness of the ibex in bringing forth young. For protection, the ibex young are usually born in March on inaccessible rocky heights, but in a short period of time they are skilled enough to wander into areas with the sheerest rocks.

Magical qualities were attributed to the ibex over the centuries, and long after biblical times amulets made of their horns were used to ward off disease.

Leopard: The Hebrew word for leopard, *namer*, means 'spotted', and probably also denotes the cheetah. Leopards continue to survive in Israel, living in the forests of the Galilee, Ein Gedi, and in the Negev desert. The Prophet

Jeremiah (13:23) mentions the spotted pelt—
"Can the leopard change his spots?"—which
was highly valued for rugs and saddle covers.

For the most part, the Bible depicts leopards
as ferocious. Daniel (7:6) uses the word leopard
to depict a four-headed, four-winged apocalyptic monster. The Bible uses the leopard in its
description of the Messianic era as portrayed
in the Book of Isaiah—"The leopard will lie
down with the kid" (Jer. 5:6)—providing an
image of a leopard watching over a city, wait-
ing to tear people to pieces.

Perhaps when the Prophet Habakkuk (1:8)
tells of horses "swifter than leopards," he may
have had the cheetah in mind.

Lion: In biblical times lions roamed throughout ancient Israel. Mentioned over 100 times
throughout the Bible, today the lion is extinct
in Israel. A symbol of purity in the ancient
Near East, the lion was used as the emblem of
the tribe of Judah. Today it is often found
embroidered on synagogue ark curtains and
Torah mantles.

The Bible does not mention lion hunting as a
sport. In the image used in the Book of Psalms
(35:17), only the helpless woman needed rescu-
ing from the lion.

Lions that ate humans were probably rare.
More common were lions that mauled people:

"As a young lion . . . I will tear and go away, and one shall rescue him" (Hos. 5:14). In one of the Bible's numerous miracle stories, Daniel is cast into a den of lions and manages to escape unharmed (Dan. 6:16–24).

Because the lion was less feared than admired, it is seldom used as a symbol of evil. Indeed, the Book of Proverbs (28:1) asserts that "the righteous are bold as a lion."

Sometimes the lion is used to represent strong enemies: "The sword shall devour the young lion" (Neh. 2:13); ". . . a voice of the roaring of young lions; for the pride of Jordan is spoiled" (Zech. 11:3).

King Solomon's Temple (1 Kings 7:29) had columns decorated with lions. Two flanked his throne, and twelve lions adorned the six steps leading up to it.

Ox: The primary reason for the domestication of wild oxen was for meat. Later the cows were used for milking and the bulls for draught purposes, which greatly increased the area of land that could be cultivated.

Several humanitarian rules about oxen are recorded in the Bible. For example, they were included in the Sabbath rest (Exod. 23:12). A straying ox should be led to safety (Exod. 23:4). These precepts clearly show a concern for animal welfare still unknown in many countries.

Oxen were offered on the altar as sacrifices (Lev. 17:3–4). The ox was a sacred animal, especially to the Egyptians and the Babylonians, and the Israelites had to be weaned away from such pagan worship.

Some oxen are described in the Bible as having the ability to gore and cause death: "If an ox gore a man or a woman . . ." (Exod. 21:28) is one such example.

Perhaps the strangest rite related to this animal was that of the red heifer used to purify ritual defilement: "Whoever touches the body of any human being shall be unclean for seven days; he shall purify himself with the water on the third day and on the seventh day, and then he will be clean again" (Num. 19:11–13). Ironically, the necessary handling of the ashes of the red heifer used to cleanse their congregations from defilement by contact with the dead rendered the priests unclean.

Some have conjectured that the use of female animals (although sacrificial animals were usually males) symbolized the imparting of new life to those who had been defiled by contact with death. The color red, being the color of blood, may have been the token of life.

Pig: The children of Israel were prohibited

by God from eating pig (Lev. 11:7 and Deut. 14:8). Some conjectured that this was for hygienic reasons. First, the pig as a frequent scavenger may pick up diseased material and either carry infection mechanically or itself become infected. Secondly, the pig is host of the tapeworm trichinosis; this passes into the muscles of a pig and can be transmitted only by being eaten. The tapeworm then invades various tissues in humans and can even cause death.

It appears from Isaiah (65:4 and 66:3,17) that during exilic times in Babylonia some Israelites brought pig's blood as an oblation in sacrifices and consumed its meat on such occasions. The Egyptians ate or sacrificed swine at full-moon festivals since, according to their mythology, the god Seth was identified with the swine. What brought about the Israelites' particularly strong aversion to pigs cannot be determined with certainty. In Maccabean times it had become a strong symbol of anti-Judaism (1 Macc. 1:44). In Christian Scriptures swine were connected with demons.

Sheep: The importance of domestic sheep to the Israelites is shown by its being mentioned some 400 times throughout the Bible. Sheep were first domesticated for their meat and fat. The wool was developed by careful breeding and became very valuable.

It is clear from Genesis (30:32) that sheep were of various colors and patterns. Throughout the Bible, sheep have deep metaphorical significance, often portrayed as a symbol of a person, helpless and easily led astray and lost. For instance, Isaiah (53:6) proclaims: "All we like sheep have gone astray; we have turned every one to his own way."

The paschal lamb is central to the festival of Passover. Sheep also appear in a festive occasion described in 1 Samuel (25:2–8), where we read about the custom of sheepshearing, which had been elevated to the rank of a festival.

Wolf: In biblical times wolves were common enough to be a major threat to flocks. "Evening wolves" (Hab. 1:8) and a "wolf of the evening" accurately describes the wolf's nocturnal habits and its tendency to howl in the evening.

In the Bible, wolves appear as preying on sheep, leaping into a flock, and scattering it so that the younger are left vulnerable (Gen. 49:27). More than half of the Bible's references to wolves link them to sheep.

While the Bible mentions men killing bears and lions, nowhere does it mention anyone killing a wolf. Not only that, but it seems to be taken for granted that the wolf is always going to capture the lamb. Since the wolf is usually represented as fierce and savage (Hab. 1:), it is used as a favorite symbol for corrupt rulers and enemies, as in "Her princes are like wolves" (Gen. 49:27; Jer. 5:6).

The wolf was also an admired animal—"more sharp-eyed than desert wolves," said Habakkuk (1:8). The Hebrew name *z'ev* (wolf) appears in the Bible (Judg. 7:25) and is still a popular Hebrew name used for boys.

Birds, Insects, Reptiles, and Fish in the Bible

BIRDS

Of the birds called by the collective name of *tzippor* or *oaf*, there are more than 350 species in the Bible. Constituting as they did an important food source, birds were regularly hunted. According to the Encyclopedia Judaica vol. 3, 37, specific birds are mentioned in the Bible.

The eggs of wild birds were often collected for food (Deut. 22:6). The snaring of birds is frequently referred to in the Bible in an allegorical way, representing a person who becomes entangled in difficulties.

The Bible makes no mention of the breeding of birds except for doves, which together with sparrows were used for various sacrificial rites, including the purification rites of a leper (Lev. 14:4).

One of the earliest bird missions in the Bible

appears in the story of Noah and the Flood. At
the end of forty days, Noah selects a raven that
he sends forth from the ark in order to determine when it would be safe to leave the ark.
The raven was most likely chosen because it is
a bird of prey, and if the earth were dry it
would be able to sustain itself by feeding on
carrion. The raven soon returns to the ark.
Later on, Noah sends forth a dove, who returns
to the ark in the first week. After a second
week the dove is again sent forth and this time
returns with an olive branch in its mouth.
Noah now was certain that the waters had
abated from the earth.

Many descriptions, parables, and allegories
taken from bird life occur in the Bible, including the beauty of the dove, the cruelty of the
eagle, and the desolation symbolized by the
owl. Ecclesiastes (12:4) mentions the singing of
birds, while the law of Deuteronomy (22:6) forbids the taking of a mother bird along with its
young. Following are some of the more noteworthy birds appearing in the Bible:

Dove and Pigeon: Several species of the dove
and the pigeon are found in Israel. It is hypoth-
esized that the Hebrew word for dove, *yonah*, is
derived from either the word *yanah* meaning to
oppress or from *anah* meaning to mourn. Isaiah
(38:14) asserts, "I do moan as a dove," while

Ezekiel (7:16) refers to "the doves of the valleys, all of them moaning."

The dove first figures into the Bible in the Noah story (Gen. 8), when Noah sends forth a dove in order to determine whether the waters had abated. When the dove returns with an olive branch in its mouth, Noah realizes that it is safe to leave the ark.

Doves were known for their strong flight, as attested to in the verse in Psalms (55:7), "Oh that I had wings like a dove." Song of Songs (6:9) alludes to the beautiful voice of the dove in the verse that asserts ". . . let me hear your voice, for it is sweet . . . ."

Turtle doves were used extensively in sacrifices. They were considered the poor person's offering (Lev. 5:7) and used when a person could not afford the more costly lamb.

The dove is the most inoffensive of birds. Though attacked by other birds, it never attacks in return. It is a symbol of Israel, say the rabbis, teaching the offerer that one should rather be of the persecuted than of those that persecute.

Eagle: Many references to the eagle can be found throughout the Bible. One of the metaphoric uses of the eagle can be found in Exodus (19:4): "You have seen what I did to the Egyptians, how I bore you on eagles' wings and

brought you to Me." Eagles are known to protect their young by flying high in the sky. This
image was dramatically concretized when in
1949 the Jews of Yemen, in southern Arabia,
were transported en masse to Israel. Many
believed their journey "on eagles wings" to be
a literal fulfillment of the biblical statement.

In the view of the commentator the Rashbam,
the eagle metaphor emphasizes the speed and
safety of God's deliverance. According to Rashi,
all other birds clutch their young between
their legs underneath because they are afraid
of another bird over-flying them. The eagle,
however, is afraid only of the hunter's arrow,
since no other bird can fly higher than it. It
therefore places its young on top of its wings,
saying: "Let the arrow rather pierce me than
my young."

The Book of Obadiah (1:4) also recounts the
ability of the eagle to fly high in the heavens:
"Though you soar alot like the eagle and set
your nest among the stars, thence will I bring
you down, says God."

The care of the eagle towards its fledglings
can be further attested to from the verse in the
farewell song of Moses (Deut. 32:11): ". . . as an
eagle that stirs up its nest hovers over its
young, spreads abroad its wings, takes them
beneath them on its pinions."

The Bible also refers to the eagle in its old age. The Book of Psalms (103:5) asserts that eagles retain their vigor in their old age: "Who satisfies your old age with good things, so that your youth is renewed like the eagle."

Fowl: Fowl generally refers to birds that are used for consumption, such as hens and cocks. In the Bible they often appear in connection with instruments used to trap them. For instance, in the Book of Hosea (7:12) we read that "even as they go, I will spread my net upon them and bring them down as the fowls of the heaven." Amos (3:5) asks the rhetorical question: "Will a snare spring up from the ground and take nothing at all?" Thus it appears that there were indeed bird hunters in biblical times.

Hawk: The hawk is referred to in Leviticus (11:16) and Deuteronomy (14:15) as one of the unclean animals that Israelites are forbidden to eat. As a migratory bird it is described for its swift flight in the Book of Job (39:26): "Does the hawk soar by your wisdom and stretch its wings toward the south?"

Hoopoe: This bird is mentioned twice in the Bible (Lev. 11:19; Deut. 14:18) as an unclean bird. The hoopoe is known for its slender decurved bill and lush plumage.

Ostrich: One of the clearest descriptions of

the ostrich is that found in Job (39:13–18): "The wing of the ostrich beats joyously, and her pinions and plumage are like the stork's. She leaves her eggs on the ground, letting them warm in the dirt, forgetting they may be crushed underfoot or trampled by a wild beast. Her young are cruelly abandoned as if they were not hers; her labor is in vain for lack of concern. God deprived her of wisdom and gave her no share of understanding, else she would soar on high, scoffing at the horse and its rider."

Owl: The owl is a nocturnal bird of prey. It appears eight times in the Bible by four different Hebrew words. *Bat hayaanah* is found in Leviticus (11:16) and in Deuteronomy (14:15), listing it as a bird forbidden to be eaten. The word *kos*, the next member of the owl family, is found in Leviticus (11:17) and in Deuteronomy (14:16). This term for owl has generally been understood to mean little owl, the smallest of its species.

The term *yanshuf* for owl (Lev. 11:17; Deut. 14:16) is derived from the Hebrew word *neshef*, meaning 'twilight', the time when the nocturnal owl hunts for its food. Finally, the Hebrew word *tinshemet* (Lev. 11:18; Deut. 14:16) is derived from the Hebrew root *nasham*, meaning 'to pant'.

Partridge: The partridge has been a popularly hunted game bird. King David complains (I Sam. 26:20) that King Saul is hunting him when he says: "For the King of Israel has come out to seek a single flea—as if he were hunting a partridge in the hills."

The Prophet Jeremiah (17:11–13) uses the partridge to illustrate the improper gathering of wealth: "Like a partridge hatching what she did not lay, so is one who amasses wealth by unjust means. In the middle of life it will leave him, and in the end he will be proven a fool."

Peacock: Noted for its beautiful rainbow-colored plumage, the peacock is found in 1 Kings (10:22) and in 2 Chronicles (9:21). Its citation in the Book of Kings suggests that Solomon had traffic with Ceylon or India, the original home of the domestic fowl, and he could therefore have introduced them.

Quail: Quail is mentioned in Exodus (16:13), Numbers (11:31–32), Psalms (1–5:40), and Psalms (78:26–30). Almost the smallest of all of the game birds, it is described in Exodus (16:13): "In the evening quails came up and covered the camp. Quails are migrants, and at certain seasons travel in large flocks a meter or two above the ground. Their migrations take them across the route followed after the Exodus from Egypt. When they are exhausted they often fall to the earth, only to be picked up by the Arabs to be eaten as a delicacy, just as they were for the ancient Israelites on their journey through the wilderness.

Raven: The raven, a black, dark-colored bird, was the first animal sent forth from Noah's ark. Its quick return was an indication that the waters had yet to abate.

In the First Book of Kings (17:4), God commanded the ravens to feed Elijah morning and evening when he hid from Ahab.

In Song of Songs (5:11) we read that "his locks are curled and black as a raven," attesting to the raven's dark color.

Stork: The white stork is one of the most striking migratory birds of Israel, slowly traveling north, especially along the Jordan Valley in March and in April. The stork is mentioned in Leviticus (11:19) and in Deuteronomy (14:18) as an unclean bird that Israelites are not permitted to eat. As a migratory bird, "the stork in heaven knows her appointed times" (Jer. 8:7). In Zechariah (5:9), the reference "the wind was in their wings" indicates that the oversized wings of a stork produced a large bellowing sound when they flapped in the air.

INSECTS

Insects are frequently mentioned in the Bible, comprising almost three quarters of all the species of the world. The great majority of them are injurious to vegetation and carriers of diseases.

Of the insects, the most referred to in the Bible are various species of the grasshopper and locust, which were notorious for the havoc that they caused to agriculture. Some varieties, however, were also permitted for food.

Among the common agricultural pests in the Bible are insects that belong to the species of beetles, fruit flies, and ants. Species of the moth are mentioned as injurious to clothing. Also troublesome to humans were the fly, gnat, louse, and flea. The bee and hornet were regarded as dangerous to people, although the latter produces honey, a prized possession for its food. Spiders and scorpions are also mentioned in the Bible, as are worms and snails. The following are some of the noteworthy biblical bugs and insects:

Ant: Ants vary widely in size and habits, but are all social, living in colonies of a dozen or so to hundreds of thousands. The ant (conjectured to be the harvester ant, sometimes called the agricultural ant) is featured in two well-known texts in Proverbs (6:6; 30:25). In both texts the ant is praised for its agility, proficiency, and deftness: "Go to the ant, you sluggard, consider her ways and be wise: which having no chief overseer or ruler provides her bread in the summer and gathers her food in the harvest" (Prov. 6:6). This type of ant collects seeds of many kinds, especially grasses, during spring and early summer and stores them in underground galleries, thus displaying their great wisdom.

In Proverbs (30:25), we again see the praiseworthiness of ants: "There are four things which are small upon the earth but they are very wise. The ants are a people not strong, yet they provide their food in the summer."

Bee: Bees are insects with complex social organization. Numerous kinds are found in Israel and of these the most important is the honey bee, for until the eighteenth century honey was the basic material for sweetening. Numerous references to honey in the Bible imply that its use was common and widespread. It is likely that much of the honey was produced by wild bees nesting in hollow trees or rocky holes, but from very early times bees have been encouraged to occupy simple hives of basket or earthenware.

In Deuteronomy (1:44) the wild bee is compared to a militant army. In the Book of Judges (14:8) a swarm of bees is found in the body of a lion carcass.

The Hebrew word for honey, *devash*, is found in more than forty different places in the Bible. Interestingly, the land of Israel itself was figuratively described in the Bible as a land of great abundance, using the words "the land flowing from milk and honey." The Hebrew word for bee, *devorah*, was the name of Deborah, the well-known judge and prophet in biblical times. Even today, Devorah continues to be a popular Hebrew name for girls.

Fly: Whereas the Bible says that flies are so annoying that they seem able to devour people, the chief point of mentioning them is not to describe them as pests but to emphasize that God had power over them. This was of the utmost importance because Baalzebub, the Canaanite Lord of the Flies, was believed to be sole creator and controller of the flies. Thus, when the Israelites went into the land of Canaan, God is shown sending a swarm of flies upon Pharaoh and his servants. Later, when Pharaoh promised to let the Israelites go, God removed the flies (Exod. 8:21–310).

In Isaiah (7:18), God calls for the flies, which swarm out of the rivers to alight in the barren valleys and in the rocky crags. Similar power to control flies is described in Psalms (78:45): "God inflicted upon them swarms of flies to devour them."

A final biblical reference to flies (Eccles. 10:1) does not mention the Canaanite god Baal-zebub directly by name. Rather it describes a stinking ointment made with dead flies, apparently used in religious rites dedicated to Baal-zebub.

Grasshopper: The grasshopper is known for its ability to jump, which is confirmed by a biblical reference in Leviticus (11:21) where we read that "they have jointed legs above their feet with which to leap upon the earth." Almost all insects and creeping things were forbidden as food, except for the grasshopper (Lev. 11:21).

In the Book of Numbers (13:33) grasshoppers were mentioned by the spies in the following manner: "We were in our own eyes as grasshoppers, so we must have been in their eyes." The reference here relates to the perception of the enemy in the eyes of the spies. The enemy was giant-sized compared to the tiny grasshopper, representative of the spies.

The unimportance of people is compared to

that of grasshoppers in the Book of Isaiah (40:22): "It is He that sits above the circle of the earth and the inhabitants thereof are as grasshoppers."

Hornet: The hornet is a savage large colonial wasp that is mentioned three times in the Bible: Exodus (23:28), Deuteronomy (7:20), and Joshua (24:12). It is known for its painful and dangerous sting. Hornets are still common in Israel, including some inhabiting the desert around the Dead Sea.

In Exodus (23:28) the Bible states: "I will send hornets ahead of you, and it shall drive you before you the Hivites, the Canaanites, and the Hittites." The other biblical references are similar in nature, relating to the destructive nature of the hornet's sting.

Locust: Perhaps no insect was more feared, or depicted more often in the Bible, than the locust. The Hebrew use of several words for locust has confused translators. For instance, in detailing the four edible flying insects that leaped (Lev. 11:22), translators listed locust, bald locust, grasshopper, and even beetle. However, as most beetles do not leap, some translators inserted "cricket" instead.

Normally locusts develop long wings and a solitary lifestyle, and are no more bothersome than other crop-eating insects. This may be why in some instances that the Bible suggests that locusts are helpless and timid, such as in Job (39:20) when they are called "afraid."

Characteristic of migration is that the locusts swarm, fly a leg of their journey, and then settle with a tremendous appetite to gather strength in order to fly again. The Bible says that they become a burden (Eccles. 12:5), a plague (1 Kings 8:37), and an evil (2 Chron. 6:28).

The most graphic descriptions of destruction by locusts are found in the biblical books of Exodus and Isaiah. Exodus (10:12–19) tells how the locust fell upon the Egyptians in such great numbers that no green thing was left in the land. Isaiah (40:22) says the insects stretched across the skies like a curtain, spreading out so that one felt secluded as in a dark tent. It is a known fact that the migratory locust does fly in such swarms as to blacken an entire sky.

The migratory phenomenon of locusts so impressed the ancients that the very word "locust" became synonymous with an invasion of uncountable numbers. The Midianites overrunning the Israelites with their cattle and tents "came as grasshoppers [locusts] for multitude" (Judg. 6:5).

While the sound of a single locust eating is inaudible, the working jaws of a swarm create a unique crackle that Joel (1:6) compared to "the teeth of a lion." Joel describes the locust as a great army that leaps across mountaintops, their wings making a terrible noise like that of a roaring fire. Here is the description in Joel's own words: "They charge like warriors, they advance like fighters, each on his own track, no tangling of paths. None pushes his fellow, each follows his own line. They burst through weapons unbroken, they rush on the city, run over the walls, climb into the houses, and enter the windows like thieves" (Joel 2:7–9).

Louse: Lice, mentioned in Exodus (8), is the third plague that God brought upon the Egyptians. The Egyptian magicians were not able to produce lice using their own magic, which caused them to say "this is the finger of God" (Exod. 8:15).

Moth: There are hundreds of varieties of moths and butterflies in Israel. Dismay at finding clothes and other possessions moth-eaten is graphically described in the Bible. Moths are judged to be destructive in a slow and treacherous way. For instance, to punish Ephraim for its iniquity, God promises to be as thoroughly destructive as a moth. Isaiah (50:9) can find no better words for warning enemies of what will happen than to describe them as eaten by moths like an old garment.

Moths are often associated with something

insubstantial. Job (27:18) speaks disdainfully of building a house as a moth does and of flimsy houses that can be crushed by a moth (27:18). In Psalms (39:11), beauty is said to be consumed like a moth.

Scorpion: Although a species of scorpion inhabiting the Sahara Desert inflicts a sting that can quickly kill a person, the species found in Israel generally does not inflict lethal stings. As a desert creature the scorpion is mentioned once in the Five Books of Moses: ". . . who led you through the great and dreadful wilderness wherein there were fiery serpents and scorpions" (Deut. 8:15).

In other biblical passages the scorpion is used symbolically or metaphorically. King Rehoboam warns the people with this statement: "My father admonished you with whips, but I will chastise you with scorpions" (1 Kings 12:11). In Ezekiel (2:6) the scorpion is used metaphorically to symbolize wicked people when God warns the people not to be afraid of scorpions.

Scorpions also played frightening roles in the mythologies of people surrounding the Israelites. In an Egyptian story the evil god Set disguised himself as a scorpion to kill the good god Horus.

Spider: The spider (*achavish*) is cited three times in the Bible. In Isaiah (59:5,6) we read of the "wicked who hatch basilisk's eggs and weave the spider's web." In the Book of Job (8:14) we learn of the tenuousness of a spider's web: ". . . whose confidence is gossamer, and whose trust is a spider's web." In Psalms (140:4), we read that "they sharpen their tongues like serpents, spiders' poison is on their lips."

Worm: There are several references to worms in the Bible. For instance, in Psalms (22:7) it says "I am a worm and no man." This verse attests to the fact that King David, in his modesty, considered that he was not worthy to really be called a man. In a verse in the Book of Isaiah (41:14) Israel as a nation is compared to a worm: "Fear not, you worm O Jacob, and you men of Israel."

REPTILES AND CREEPING THINGS

The Five Books of Moses define reptiles as "every swarming thing that swarms upon the earth . . . whatsoever goes upon the belly, and whatsoever goes upon all fours" (Lev. 11:41–42). This embraces all species of reptiles, including snakes, crocodiles, as well as certain species of the lizard, gecko, skink, chameleon, and monitor. Of these last five genera, the Bible enumerates six species of swarming things to which particularly severe laws of uncleanliness apply (Lev. 11:29–39). Among the reptiles, crocodiles and snakes are extensively described.

Several times the Bible mentions gigantic legendary reptiles that were said to have rebelled against the Creator, who was ultimately compelled to wage war over them. These will be described in a chapter devoted to Fantastic Beasts.

Following is a description of a cross section of some of the most noteworthy biblical reptiles:

Chameleon: Chameleons of Israel are small and agile, able to easily climb trees and walls. Their skins change to various hues of green-gray and brown, based on a combination of light, temperature, and emotional factors. Whether they are really mentioned in the Bible is up for conjecture. In the listing of creeping things unclean to eat (Lev. 11:30), some biblical translations give chameleon as one of the three lizard-types of creatures.

Crocodile: In Egypt crocodiles were sacred to Set, a god of evil. Even mummies of crocodiles have been found in several Egyptian cemeteries.

The Bible uses no word specifically for crocodile, but some of the references to dragons, monsters, or the Leviathan (Job 41) undoubtedly describe it, especially when the monster is used as a symbol of Egypt. For example, in Ezekiel (29:3) we read of "Pharaoh, King of Egypt, the great dragon that lies in the midst of the rivers." Here Pharaoh himself is symbolized as the great crocodile.

Frog: When the Israelites were in slavery in Egypt, God sent frogs as one of the Ten Plagues (Exod. 8:2). After the frogs had covered the land, Pharaoh sent for Moses and asked that he have God return the frogs to the river. Instead, God killed the frogs so that they dropped dead all over the Egyptian villages.

Lizard: The Hebrew word for lizard was a general term for a number of species. Lizards were by far the most conspicuous of the eight reptiles in ancient Israel that creep on the earth and defile, as mentioned in Leviticus (11:29–30). Because the lizard is somewhat resemblant of the serpent, it continues to be disliked, although it is useful for its ability to destroy insects.

Snake: Almost the only positive thing that the Bible has to say about snakes is in the Book of Proverbs (30:19), where the serpent is admired for its grace and movement. Every place else, the Bible has only abhorrence for the serpent.

Because Israel's neighbors associated the serpent with an earth mother, it is not surprising to find the serpent with Eve at the very beginning of Genesis 3. But while other peoples had the snake play a beneficial role in fertility cults, the biblical snake is continually used to represent temptation and the power of evil. The biblical disparagement of the snake may be due to the fact that snakes played a prominent role in the religions of Israel's neighbors. In Egypt, for example, Re was primary among several gods identified with the serpent, and pharaohs had the image of a cobra on their crown. Because of the prevalence of snake worship, the Israelites were forced to establish the supremacy of God by emphasizing that God had created snakes (Job 26:13) and their poison (Deut. 32:24). Once having created snakes, God retained power over them (Ps. 91:13). Even if a person should try to hide in the bottom of the sea, God could command serpents to follow and strike him there (Amos 9:3).

The bite of a dangerous snake was always a concern to humans. According to the Bible, snakes will bite you if you are on a path (Gen. 49:17), if you disturb a hedge that they are hiding in (Eccles. 10:8), if they are not enchanted by snake charmers (Eccles. 10:11), or if God commands them to attack (Deut. 32:24).

Almost everything evil in the Bible is compared to the poisonous snake. Wicked people "suck the poison of asps" (Job 20:16) and contain the "gall of asps within" (Job 20:14).

Entire populations who will not listen to the word of God, such as Babylon in Isaiah (14), are compared to serpents. Jeremiah (46:22–23) predicts that the voice of Egypt "shall go like a serpent."

Since the Israelites often had to camp at oases, snakes that were in those vicinities were a true problem for them. Perhaps that is why a well on the west side of Jerusalem was later called Dragon's Spring (Neh. 2:13) and *zohelet* (a word for 'serpent') was the name given to rocks near springs at En Rogel (1 Kings 1:9).

Which poisonous snakes the Israelites encountered is not clear. It is most likely that the venomous snakes of the Bible would have either been vipers, which have long movable fangs, or cobras, which have short stationary fangs.

One of the most interesting snake narratives in the Five Books of Moses is that related to the performance of snake tricks, both by Pharaoh's magicians as well as by Aaron. In Exodus (7:8–12) Moses demonstrates God's power by having Aaron, pursuant to God's instructions, cast a staff onto the ground, which immediately turns into a snake. Pharaoh then summons his wise men, sorcerers and magicians, who are also able to perform the same trick. However, Aaron's staff-turned-snake swallows the staff-turned-snakes of the Egyptians. Biblical commentators believe that the trick depends upon a particular species of snake called the *naja haje*, or 'Egyptian cobra'. A peculiarity of this snake is that it can be made motionless by pressure just below the head. Thus temporarily paralyzed, the cobra becomes rigid, like a stick, but when it is thrown on the ground, it is jolted back into action.

Photographs have been taken showing how closely the rigid snake resembles a stick, and instances have been reported where modern Egyptian magicians allow bystanders to handle "charmed" snakes with impunity. All this forms a link with the ancient wizardry that flourished under the rule of the pharaohs.

Ancient sorcerers who performed the snake trick probably carried staffs of similar size and shape to the rigid cobra. By substituting a paralyzed snake at the proper time, it could still be shown as an ordinary stick up to the moment it was thrown to the ground. The fiery "flying" serpent described in Isaiah (30:6) might be a cobra, since—with a little imagination—the inflated hood might look like wings. However, "flying" would also certainly describe the rapid strike made by vipers.

Tortoise: The tortoise is mentioned once in the Bible in Leviticus (11:29). Some have said that the tortoise that some scholars refer to in Leviticus as a forbidden animal is actually a lizard. As for turtles such as the "voice of the turtle" that is heard in the spring (Song of Songs 2:12), these are not reptiles but rather turtledoves.

FISH

Fish are often mentioned in the Bible, where they are referred to by the collective term *dagim*. It is likely that fish constituted an important food in biblical times. Reference to their increasing number in the "Great Sea" is found in Ezekiel (47:10), and in Jerusalem, one of the gates was called the Fish Gate (Zeph. 1:10). The rapid multiplication of fish gave rise to a verb *dagah*, meaning 'to teem' (Gen. 48:16).

Although the Bible does not mention any fish by name, it has more than a dozen terms for fishing implements: *choach*—'hook' (Job 40:26); *chakah*—'fish hook' (Job 40:25); *mishmeret*— 'fishing net' (Isa. 19:8). The importance of fish in the economy of Israel is reflected in the vision of the Prophet Ezekiel (47:10) of the desalination of the waters of the Dead Sea: "And it shall come to pass that fishers shall stand by it from En Gedi to En Eglaim. There shall be a place for the spreading of nets."

The Bible mentions Egypt as a place where fish were plentiful (Num. 11:5). Deuteronomy (4:18) forbids making images of fish for worship. The pagan fish goddess Atargatis was worshipped at Ashkelon and among the Nabateans.

People suffering misfortune (Eccles. 9:12) or captured by enemies (Hab. 1:15) are compared to fish caught in a net. Fishing is used in the Bible as a figure of God's judgment on nations or individuals. "I am sending for many fishermen," declares God, "and they shall haul them out . . ." (Jer. 16:16), and "I will cast My net over you . . ." (Ezek. 32:3).

In the Bible a distinction is made between fish that are permitted as food and those that are forbidden. Forbidden fish were those that did not have fins and scales.

The largest fish mentioned in the Bible is the

dag gadol in the Book of Jonah, which swallowed him up for three days. It has often been conjectured that the large fish referred to in this book is a whale and not a fish.

SUMMARY CHART OF ANIMALS APPEARING IN THE BIBLE AND THE TALMUD

English Name	Hebrew Name	Reference
Addax	Yachmor	Deut. 14:5
Ant	Gimala	Prov. 6:6–8
Ass	Chamor	Gen. 12:16
	Ayeer	Gen. 32:16
	Atone	Judg. 5:10
Bat	Atalef	Lev. 11:19
Bear	Dov	1 Sam. 17:34–37
Bee	Devorah	Deut. 1:44
Beetle	Tola'at	Jon. 4:7
Bison	Te'oh	Deut. 14:15
Boar	Chazeer Meeya'ar	Ps. 80:14
Buffalo	Miree	2 Sam. 6:13
Bug	Peeshpaysh	Ter. 8:2
Buzzard	Ayah	Lev. 11:14
	Ra'ah	Deut. 14:13
	Guss	Chullin 3:1
Camel	Gamal	Gen. 12:16
	Becher	Isa. 60:6
	Na'akah	Shabbat 5:1

English Name	Hebrew Name	Reference
Cattle	Bakar	Gen. 13:5
	Shor	Gen. 32:6
	Alafeem	Deut. 7:13
	Abeereem	Isa. 34:7
	Par	Gen. 32:16
	Eygel	Gen. 15:9
Centipede	Marbey Raglayim	Lev. 11:42
	Nadal	Mikva'ot 5:3
Chameleon	Teenshemet	Lev. 11:30
Cheetah	Bardilus	Baba Kamma 1:4
Cobra	Peten	Deut. 32:33
	Saraf	Num. 21:6
Cock	Sechvee	Job 38:36
Corals	Peneeneem	Lam. 4:7
Crane	Agoor	Isa. 38:14
Cricket	Tzelatzal	Deut. 28:42
Crimson Worm	Tola'at Shanee	Exod. 25:4
Crocodile	Taneen	Exod. 7:9
	Leviyatan	Job 40:25
Deer	Yachmoor	Deut. 14:5
	Ayal	Deut. 14:5
Dog	Kelev	Exod. 22:30
Dove	Yonah	Gen. 8:8
Eagle	Ayeet	Gen. 15:11
Earthworm	Tola'at	Isa. 14:11
Elephant	Peel	Kilayim 8,6
Fish	Dag	Jon. 2:1
Flea	Parosh	1 Sam. 21:14
Fly	Yavchoosh	Niddarim 3:2
Fox	Shu'al	Lam. 5:18
Frog	Tzefardaya	Exod. 7:27
Gazelle	Tzvee	Deut. 12:15

English Name	Hebrew Name	Reference
Gecko	Anaka	Lev. 11:30
Gnat	Arov	Exod. 8:17
Goat	Ayz	Lev. 7:23
	Se'eer	Gen. 37:31
	Tayeesh	Gen. 30:35
Goat (wild)	Akoo	Deut. 14:15
Goose	Barboor	1 Kings 5:3
	Avaz	Shabbat 24:3
Grasshopper	Chargol	Lev. 11:22
	Chagav	Num. 13:33
	Salam	Lev. 11:22
Gull	Shachaf	Lev. 11:16
Hare	Arnevet	Lev. 11:6
Hawk	Naytz	Lev. 11:16
Heron	Anafa	Lev. 11:19
Hippopotamus	Behemot	Job 40:15
Horse	Soos	Exod. 9:3
Hyena	Tzavoah	1 Sam. 13:18
Hyrax	Shafan	Lev. 11:5
Ibex	Ya'el	Ps. 104:18
Jackal	Shu'al	Judg. 15:4
Kestrel	Tachmas	Lev. 11:16
Kite	Da'ah	Lev. 11:14
Leech	Alooka	Prov. 30:15
Leopard	Namer	Isa. 11:6
Lion	Aree	Isa. 38:13
	Aryeh	Gen. 49:9
	Kefeer	Ezek. 19:3
	Lavee	Gen. 49:9
	Layish	Job 4:11
	Shachal	Hos. 5:14

English Name	Hebrew Name	Reference
Lizard	Li'ta'ah	Lev. 11:30
	Tzav	Lev. 11:29
Locust	Arbeh	Exod. 10:11
	Gazam	Amos 4:9
	Govai	Amos 7:1
	Chasil	1 Kings 8:37
	Yelek	Jer. 51:14
Louse	Ken Keenem	Isa. 51:6
	Keenam	Exod. 8:13
Mackerel	Kolias Haeespaneem	Shabbat 22:2
Maggot	Reema	Exod. 16:24
Mole Rat	Chafarparot	Isa. 2:20
	Eeshut	Kelim 21:3
Mongoose	Nimeeya	Baba Batra 2:5
Monkey	Kof	1 Kings 10:22
Moth	Nosays	Isa. 10:18
	Sas	Isa. 51:8
	Ash	Isa. 50:9
Mouse	Achbar	Lev. 11:29
Mule	Pered	Isa. 66:20
Nightingale	Zamir	Song of Songs 2:12
Onager	Arod	Job 39:5
Oryx	Zemer	Deut. 14:5
Ostrich	Ya'en	Lam. 4:3
Owl	Oa'ach	Isa. 13:21
	Bat Ya'anah	Lev. 11:16
	Shalach	Lev. 11:17
Ox	Re'em	Numb. 23:22
Partridge	Chaglah	Numb. 26:33
	Koray	1 Sam. 26:20
Peacock	Tookee	1 Kings 10:22
Porcupine	Koopad	Kilayim 8:5
Quail	Slav	Exod. 16:13

English Name	Hebrew Name	Reference
Rat	Choled	Lev. 11:29
	Chulda	Kelim 15:6
Raven	Orev	Gen. 8:7
Sardine	Tareet	Nedarim 6:4
	Cheelak	Avoda Zarah 2:6
Scorpion	Akrav	Deut. 8:15
Sheep	Tzon	Gen. 4:2
	Ayil	Gen. 22:13
	Rachel	Gen. 32:15
	Keves	Exod. 12:5
	Taleh	1 Sam. 7:9
Skink	Chomet	Lev. 11:30
Snake	Nachash	Gen. 3:1
Sparrow	Tzippor Dror	Lev. 14:4
Spider	Akaveesh	Isa. 59:5
Stork	Chasida	Lev. 11:19
Swift	Sees	Isa. 38:14
Swine	Chazeer	Lev. 11:7
Tahash	Tachash	Exod. 26:19
Turtle Dove	Tor	Gen. 15:9
Viper	Efesh	Isa. 30:6
	Shefeefon	Gen. 49:17
	Tzefesh	Isa. 14:29
	Tzeefonee	Isa. 11:8
Vulture	Peres	Lev. 11:13
	Ozneeyah	Lev. 11:13
	Racham	Lev. 11:18
	Nesher	Lev. 11:13
Wasp	Tzeera	Exod. 23:28
Whale	Leviyatan	Ps. 104:26
Wolf	Z'ev	Isa. 11:6

Animals in
Jewish Thought

With Judaism's strong emphasis on the significance of human beings, it is not surprising that many Jewish thinkers have a human-centered philosophy according to which animals were created for the purpose of serving humans. Although the Book of Genesis does not explicitly state that animals were created solely for human benefit, the creation narrative clearly describes the human as the culmination of God's creative activity, with the corollary that all creatures are subordinate to him (Gen. 1:26–28).

God said: "Let us make man in our image, after our likeness, and let him have dominion over the fish of the sea, and over the fowl of the air, and over the cattle, and over all the earth, and over every creeping thing that creeps upon the earth. . . ." And God said to them: "Be fruitful and multiply and replenish the earth, and subdue it, and have dominion over the fish of the sea, and over the fowl of the air, and over every living thing that creeps on the earth."

The philosopher Saadia Gaon, in his book *Ha'emunot Vehade'* ('Beliefs and Opinions'), presents his rationale for why God created animals and creatures other than humans. He first asserts that God simply willed it so; secondly, God created animals in order to reveal His wisdom to humankind; and thirdly, that animal creation afforded humankind many benefits.

Maimonides, on the other hand, writing in his *Guide for the Perplexed* (3:13), does not consider the question of why God created animals a particularly significant one. He asserts in his book that God willed it so and that it is incorrect to understand the Genesis narrative as implying that animals were created solely for humans.

An interesting debate between Saadia Gaon and Maimonides ensued as to whether animals go to Heaven. Saadia in his *Ha'emunot Vehade'* (III,17) argues that God does compensate animals with a share in Heaven for the suffering that they must undergo when they are slaughtered by people for food. Maimonides, on the other hand, considers the opinion that animals are rewarded with Heavenly bliss to be an alien and un-Jewish view. The Midrash (Ecclesrastes Rabbah 3:18) also reflects Maimonides's view when it asserts that hardly any attention is paid to the soul of the animal because "an animal is not mindful of what it does . . . an animal is ignorant of what leads to death and has no portion in the world to come."

There is also an obvious intellectual gap between a human's ability to rationalize and abstract and the animal, which cannot. The animal in no way can compete with humans, since the study of Torah—one of Judaism's most important religious duties—is limited to the human species, who were made in God's image.

Rabbinic literature puts forth some interesting questions and challenges in connection with the punishment of animals. In commenting on the biblical prohibition of bestiality, the Talmud Sanhedrin (54a) asks the question: "If the man has sinned, wherein has the animal sinned?"

Judah Halevi in his Kuzari (III, 11) discusses the problem of animal suffering. He asserts that we do not know the answer to this terrible problem, but since the wisdom of the Creator is evidenced in the astonishing skill with which the animals are endowed we can only bow in submission. As Judah Halevi puts it:

When an evil thought suggests that there is injustice in the circumstance that the hare falls a prey to the lion or wolf, and the fly to the spider, reason steps in warning him as follows: How can I charge the All-wise with injustice when I am convinced of this justice, and that injustice is out of the question? If the lion's pursuit of the hare and the spider's of the fly were mere accidents, I should assert the necessity of accident. I see, however, that this wise and just Manager of the World equipped the lion with the means for hunting, with ferocity, strength, teeth and claws, but He furnished the spider with cunning and taught it to weave a net which it constructs without having learned to do so; how God equipped it with the instruments required, and appointed the fly as its food just as many fishes serve other fishes for food. Can I say anything but that this is the fruit of a wisdom which I am unable to grasp, and that I must submit to God who is called "The Rock"—God's deeds are perfect.

In poetic passages in the rabbinic literature, however, it is suggested that animals exist solely for man. Thus, Genesis Rabbah (8:6) asserts that mammals, birds, and fish were created on the analogy of a king who had a tower stocked with all good things. If he receives no guests, what pleasure does he derive from so stocking it? Men are God's guests, and the animals are "stocked" for his benefit.

With all of this said, one must be reminded of the important fact that Judaism teaches that cruelty to animals is strictly forbidden. People must look after the animals in their care, and according to rabbinic law feed their animals before eating themselves. Animal slaughtering must be done in ways that avoid unnecessary pain to the animal.

Regarding the use of animals for research, there is some divergence of rabbinic opinions. One view is that while there was no basis in Jewish law for a legal ban on such experiments, they were morally indefensible. Another view, refuting the former one, basically asserts that the pain of the animal surely counts less than the pain of sick people who might be helped by such experiments. This appears to be the prevailing view, provided that all reasonable steps are taken to prevent any unnecessary suffering and to limit the practice strictly to the advancement of human health.

Two major principles emerge from these rabbinic teachings. Humans are superior to the animal kingdom, and therefore animal research for the advancement of human health is permissible. Animals are to be used to benefit humans, but the pain caused to animals must be reduced to the barest minimum.

The Animal
in Jewish Ritual

In the ancient world, the pagans not only worshipped their gods but also their animals, many of which were deemed to be sacred. They often endowed animals with both divine and demonic powers, choosing to embody their gods within the forms of animals. Thus for example, the ancient Egyptians worshipped Thus, the sacred bull, as their god of fertility. Cat images abounded in Egyptian temples, since the cat was an animal sacred to the goddess Baste, and the Egyptian sun god Re was closely associated with cats. Other deified animals included the serpent Wazit and the sacred scarab beetle Ra.

In marked contrast to the pagans, the Israelites worshipped the One God, Creator of both nature and animals. The Bible outlawed any form of animal worship, as shown in the story of the golden calf in the Book of Exodus, which clearly relates Moses's abhorrence of the sin of the Israelites who built it.

The Bible does describe, however, certain rituals whose vehicle of operation include animals. Following is a brief description of animals used in biblical rituals.

SCAPEGOAT

Leviticus (16:8–10) presents a fascinating ritual related to the Day of Atonement. As part of the ritual we are told that Aaron cast lots upon two goats. One lot was for God, and the other lot was for Azazael. And Aaron presented the goat upon which the lot fell for God, and offered it for a sin offering. But the goat, on which the lot fell for Azazel, was set alive before God, to make atonement over him. It was subsequently sent away into the wilderness.

The goat that was dispatched to Azazel was not a sacrifice, since it was not slaughtered. From the biblical verses themselves it is not even clear whether the goat was killed. The goat was dispatched as a kind of vicarious atonement to carry the sins of Israel into the wilderness. Thus the people were symbolically cleansed of their sins on the Day of Atonement.

A detailed description of the ritual during Second Temple times is found in the Mishnah in the general description of the worship service of the Day of Atonement: the High Priest cast lots—upon one the word *L'YHVH* ('to the Lord') was written and upon the other *La'Azazel* ('to Azazel'). After he drew lots, on the head of the goat chosen for Azazel he bound a thread of crimson wool and stood the animal opposite the gate through which it would ultimately be taken (Talmud Yoma 4:1–2). After the High Priest had performed several other rituals he returned to the goat, placed his hands on it, and confessed the sins of the people. The goat was then banished to the wilderness. The entire ceremony has been preserved in the traditional Machzor for the High Holy Days and is a part of its liturgy.

The exact meaning of Azazel was already a point of dispute in Talmudic times. Some asserted that it was the name of the place to which the goat was sent, while others believed that it was the name of some "power." The commentators Ibn Ezra and Nachmonides both interpret Azazel as the name of the goat, and their view is also found in the Talmud Yoma (67b): "The school of Rabbi Ishmael explained that it is called Azazel because it atones for the acts of the fallen angels Uzza and Azael."

David Kimchi, in his *Book of Roots*, explains the word as meaning the name of the mountain to which the goat was taken, and the mount was so called because the goat was taken there.

There have been attempts to compare the ritual of the goat to several customs of the ancient world. For instance, in Babylon, it was customary on the festival of Akitu (New Year) to give a goat as a substitute for a human being to Ereshkigal, the goddess of the abyss. During plagues, the Hittites used to send a goat into enemy territory in order that it should carry the plague there.

The word scapegoat, which today is used to denote a person who is made to bear the blame for others, is derived from the ceremony of the goats back in biblical times.

RED HEIFER (*PARAH ADUMAH*)

The red heifer refers to the animal whose ashes were used in the ritual purification of persons and objects defiled by a corpse (Num. 19). The Bible describes that the red cow be without blemish, that it should have no defect, and that it should never have been yoked.

Unlike ordinary animal sacrifices, which could be slaughtered only at the entrance of the Tent of Meeting (Lev. 17:5), the red heifer was to be killed outside the camp. The ashes of the red heifer were to be burned with cedar wood, hyssop, and scarlet cast upon the pyre. The gathered ashes, dissolved in fresh water, were to be sprinkled on those who had become contaminated through contact with the dead.

This ordinance is one of the most mysterious in all of the Scriptures. The aim of this law was to purify the defiled, and yet it defiled all those who were in any way connected with the preparation of the ashes and the water of purification.

The need to be cleansed after touching a corpse reflected an ancient and universal fear of the dead, whose spirits were believed to be capable of injuring people. Some commentators assert that the ritual of the red heifer is doubtlessly based on pre-biblical practices. (An old Canaanite epic tells of the death of the god of fertility, who went to the underworld and there copulated with a heifer.)

The idea is clearly presented in the story of the red heifer that Israelites are a holy people and that holiness demands a state of physical and spiritual purity. Israelites must eat "clean" foods, and if they touch anything upon which a taboo rests, such as dead humans or animals unfit for food, they become tainted and must wait until a certain period has elapsed to have their pristine condition restored.

Most difficult of all the aspects of the ritual is the provision that handling the ashes renders the person impure. A Midrash (Tanchuma, Chukkat 26) relates that a gentile once came to Rabbi Yochanan ben Zakkai and asked about the reason for the ritual. The rabbi gave him a rational answer but later admitted to his students that a mystery was involved, for in and of themselves the dead were not impure nor the ashes purifying. "But," said the Sage, "this is what God has decreed, and you may not transgress Law."

In another explanation of the symbolism of the ingredients mixed with the red heifer ashes, the majestic cedar of Lebanon was said to be pride and the hyssop a symbol of humility.

The story of the red heifer is read in the synagogue on one of the Sabbaths before Passover. Its reading is meant to commemorate the purification of the unclean so that they may be enabled to bring the Passover sacrifice in a state of purity.

HEIFER WITH BROKEN NECK (*EGLAH ARUFA*)

This ritual could best be described as an expiatory ceremony for an untraceable murder. As prescribed in the Book of Deuteronomy (21:1–9), when an unsolved murder is committed in a community, the elders of the community nearest to the corpse are required to bring an unworked heifer to an uncultivated area in a watered wadi, break the heifer's neck, wash their hands over it, and profess their innocence to the bloodshed.

According to various commentators, this ritual for unsolved manslaughter was likely to have gone back to very ancient times, for there are Hittite laws resembling the biblical ritual in this respect. Underlying these provisions was the concept that the murder stained the land and that without punishment of the guilty the cultic purity of the community was impaired. The community nearest to the place of the murder was the one chosen to be responsible for carrying out the rite of the red heifer.

Commentators have written of the practical value of this rite. The ritual, it was reasoned, would attract a great deal of public attention and interest, and therefore the level of communal responsibility would be raised by this procedure, even perhaps as much as by the execution of the murderer, were he/she to be apprehended. The commentator Abarbanel, in a similar vein, asserted that the shock value of the rite would prevent the people from forgetting the act and would also keep alive the search for the perpetrator.

SACRIFICES AND BURNT OFFERINGS

In biblical times, sacrifices were generally intended to obtain God's favor and atone for the sins of the sacrificer. They also demonstrated one's submission to God and served as a recognition of God's great power. Although libation of wine and meal offerings played a prominent role in some of the rituals, the most important biblical sacrifices were those of animals. The sacrificial animal had to be free of all blemishes, domesticated, and had to be the property of the person who was offering the sacrifice. Here is a brief summary of biblical sacrifices and the animals that were used to accompany them.

Propitiatory Offerings

Two offerings belong to this category: the sin offering, called a *chattat*, and the guilt offering, called an *asham*. The sin offering was suited to the rank and the circumstance of the person who offered it. Thus, the High Priest brought a young bull (Lev. 4:3). A *nasi* ('ruler') brought a male goat (Lev. 4:23) and a commoner would bring a female goat (Lev. 4:28) or a lamb (Lev. 4:32). A sin offering of one male goat was required at each of the sacred festivals, including the New Moon (Num. 28:15), Passover (Num. 25:22–24), Shavuot (Num. 28:30), Rosh Hashanah (Num. 29:5), the Day of Atonement (Num. 29:11), and each day of the Festival of Sukkot (Num. 29:16, 19).

Rites of purification called for lesser sin offerings. For example, lambs or birds were used after childbirth (Lev. 12:6–8), leprosy (Lev. 14:12–14), and unclean issues (Lev. 15:5).

The guilt offering was a special kind of sin offering (Lev. 5:7) that was required when persons had been denied their rightful due. In addition to the reparation of the amount defrauded, plus a fine of 20 percent (Lev. 5:16–24), guilty persons had to bring a guilt offering, usually a ram.

Burnt Offerings

In Hebrew *olah*, meaning 'to go up', this sacrifice used these animals: bulls, sheep or goats, and birds (Lev. 1:3–7). A continual burnt offering (called an *olah tamid*), consisting of a male lamb that was sacrificed both morning and evening (Exod. 29:38–42), was made twice daily during biblical times. Two additional lambs were offered each Sabbath (Num. 28:9–10). There were no sin offerings that accompanied the burnt offering sacrifices. On the other hand, a sin offering of one goat was required along with the burnt offerings on the other holy days. Bulls, lambs, and rams were the primary animals used for the burnt offerings.

Peace Offerings

Called *shelamim* in Hebrew, this type of offering was the most basic of all communal sacrifices. Any domesticated animal was allowed to be used as a peace offering, which always concluded with some type of communal meal. The peace offering was specified only for the celebration of Shavuot (Lev. 23:19–20), in the ritual for the completion of a Nazirite vow (Num. 6:17–20), and at the installation of the priests (Exod. 29:19–34). National events that called for the peace offering included the successful completion of a military campaign (1 Sam. 11:15), the end of a famine (2 Sam. 24:25), and the praising of a candidate for the kingship (1 Kings 1:9).

Animal Care
in Jewish Tradition

Moral and legal rules concerning the treatment of animals are based on the principle that animals are part of God's creation toward which humans bear responsibility. Laws and other indications in the Bible make it clear not only that cruelty to animals is forbidden but also that mercy, kindness, and compassion to them are demanded of humans by God. The rabbinic name for the offense of cruelty to animals is *tz'ar ba'alei chayim* ("pain to living creatures"). Killing an animal when it is not for legitimate human need is strictly forbidden. Torturing an animal is regarded as a criminal act.

According to traditional rabbinic interpretation of the biblical record, humans were not allowed to eat meat until after the Flood, although the sacrifice of animals to God had been previously allowed. Adam, the first man,

77

was not permitted to eat meat, for he was told: "Behold, I have given you every herb yielding seed which is upon the face of the earth, and every tree, in which is the fruit of a tree yielding seed—to you it shall be for food" (Gen. 1:29). Here we clearly see that Adam, the perfect man, as an inhabitant of the Garden of Eden, which represents the ideal society, is limited to fruits and vegetables.

Not until we arrive at the story of Noah is meat permitted to be eaten: "Every moving thing that lives shall be for you; as the green herb have I given you all. Only flesh with the life thereof, which is the blood thereof, shall you not eat" (Gen. 9:1–4).

One of the so-called "seven laws of the sons of Noah" (i.e., laws that were binding, according to Judaism, on all people, non-Jews as well as Jews) is the prohibition from eating the meat of a living animal.

Both the Bible and rabbinic commentators have attached particular stress to respecting the needs and feelings of animals. The Sabbath is described as a day when the ox and the mule may also have rest, the same as humans (Exod. 20:10). The Bible prohibits muzzling of an ox when it is treading out grain (Deut. 25:4).

In view of the feelings of animals, the Bible

says: "You shall not slaughter it on the same day with its young (Lev. 22:28). Commenting on this verse, the medieval philosopher Maimonides explains (*Guide to the Perplexed* 3:48) that the pain of the animals under such circumstances is very substantial. He thus asserts that there is no difference between human suffering and the pain felt by other living beings in a case such as this.

The humanitarian motive toward the animal is also evident in the law concerning an enemy's beast of burden that must not be deserted but helped when it is seen lying prostrate under its burden (Exod. 23:5). The Bible also says: "You shall not plow with an ox and a donkey harnessed together" (Deut. 22:10), since they differ greatly in size and strength. The commentator Ibn Ezra explains that the uneven steps would cause severe discomfort to the large animal and distress to the smaller donkey. Under the Jewish legal system the punishment for muzzling a working animal is more severe than that for preventing a human laborer from eating as he works—presumably because an animal is defenseless (Tur Choshen Mishpat 338).

God Himself is often represented as being constantly concerned with providing for the needs of animals, and we are told that "the just person takes care of his beast, but the heart of the wicked is without mercy" (Prov. 12:10).

Hunting as a sport was never popular among the Jewish people. Nimrod and Esau, who were too fond of the chase, have always been regarded unfavorably in Jewish tradition. Rabbi Ezekiel Landau, a seventeenth-century sage, in one of his responsa, writes:

> The law against cruelty to animals applies in every case except where an animal is slaughtered outright, or killed for a material benefit to man . . . . In the Torah the sport of hunting is ascribed only to fierce characters like Nimrod and Esau, never to any of the patriarchs or their descendants . . . I cannot comprehend how a Jew could ever dream of killing animals merely for the pleasure of hunting . . . We may kill wild animals found in places inhabited by human beings, where the beasts constitute a menace. But it is certainly no act of merit to pursue wild beasts in their haunts. It is rather a lustful occupation . . . When the act of killing is prompted by sport, it is downright cruelty.

Yehezekel Landau, an eighteenth-century rabbi from Prague, wrote one of the classic responsa on the subject of hunting:

How can a Jew kill a living animal for no other
purpose than to satisfy cravings of his time . . .
[and if one attempts a rationalization and says]
it is because bears and wolves and other vio-
lent animals are liable to cause damage, [such
an argument might make sense] in cases when
those animals come into a human settlement . . . but to pursue them in forests, their
place of residence, when they do not want to
come to a human settlement, is no *mitzvah* and
you are only pursuing the desires of your heart.
(Noda B'Yehudah, Mahadurah Tenina)

It has been suggested that the Jewish method
of slaughtering animals for food, particularly
the laws that the knife be exceedingly sharp
and without the slightest notch, were moti-
vated by consideration for the animal because
this method is the most painless.

Another act of mercy, related this time to
birds, appears in the Book of Deuteronomy
(22:6). This is one of two commandments (the
other being to honor parents) in the entire Five
Books of Moses that presents a reward, namely
a longer life, for its performance: "If you come
across a bird's nest in a tree or on the ground,
and the nest has young birds or even eggs, and
the mother is sitting with her young, do not
take the mother together with her children. Let

the mother go and take only the young—so that you may fare well and live a long life."

According to the commentator Abarbanel, the concern here is with the preservation of the species for the long-term good of humanity (i.e., the mother must live to lay more eggs). Nachmanides, on the other hand, understands this religious obligation in terms of education to mercy: by not being allowed to take the offspring in the mother's presence, by practicing compassion to animals, we become even more compassionate to human beings. This religious obligation reminds us that animals, like human beings, can suffer emotionally. Just as we cannot wantonly cause them physical pain, so we cannot add to their mental anguish.

Two other biblical commandments reinforce this constraint: "When an ox or a sheep or a goat is born, it shall stay seven days with its mother, and from the eighth day on, it shall be acceptable as an offering by fire to God. However, no animal from the herd or from the flock shall be slaughtered on the same day with its young" (Lev. 22:27–28).

"You shall not boil a kid in its mother's milk" (Exod. 34:26).

Rabbi Samuel Raphael Hirsch, a foremost spokesperson for Orthodox Judaism in the nineteenth century in Germany, points out that this law that asks us to remember that animals and their young have a bond is a good starting point for teaching our own children compassion. Above all, those to whom the care of young minds has been entrusted should see to it that they respect both the smallest and largest animals as livings beings, which, like people, have been summoned to the joy of life.

In centuries past the Jewish people have not had the need to organize societies such as exist in general society for the prevention of cruelty to animals. The Jewish trait of compassion, nurtured by a long chain of tradition, has afforded permanent protection of animals under Jewish control.

There are many other statements and stories in Jewish tradition related to the prevention of cruelty to animals. Here are some of the more noteworthy ones:

1. You must not eat your own meal until you have seen to it that all your animals have been fed. (Talmud Berachot 40a).

2. If an animal falls into a ditch on the Sabbath, place pillows and bedding under it (since it cannot be moved until the end of the Sabbath).

3. Rabbi Judah the Prince observed a calf as it was being led to the slaughterhouse. The animal broke away from the herd and hid itself

under Rabbi Judah's clothing, crying for mercy. But Judah pushed it away saying, "Go. This is your destiny." They said in heaven, "Since he showed no compassion, we will bring suffering to him." For many years after this act, Rabbi Judah suffered a series of painful illnesses. One day, Judah's servant was sweeping the house. She was about to sweep away some young weasels that she found on the floor. "Leave them alone," Judah said to his house-keeper. Subsequently they spoke of Judah this way in heaven: "Since he has shown compassion to these rodents, we will be compassionate with him," and he was cured of his illnesses. (Talmud Baba Metzia 85a.)

4. Compassion should be extended to all crea-tures, neither destroying nor despising any of them. For God's wisdom is extended to all created things: minerals, plants, animals, and humans. This is the reason the rabbis warned us against despising food. In this way, a per-son's pity should be extended to all of the works of the Holy Blessed One, just as in God's wisdom, nothing is to be despised. One should not uproot anything which grows, unless it is necessary, nor kill any living thing unless it is necessary. And one should choose a good death for them with a knife that has been carefully examined, to have pity on them as far as pos-

sible. (Moses Cordovero, *The Palm Tree of Deborah.*)

5. Jews must avoid plucking feathers from live geese, because it is cruel to do so. (Code of Jewish Law, Even HaEzer 5:14.)

6. When animals lose their young, they suffer great pain. There is no difference between human pain and the pain of other living creatures. (Moses Maimonides, *Guide for the Perplexed* III:48.)

7. It is forbidden to tie the legs of an animal, beast, or fowl in such a way as to cause them pain and it is forbidden to make a bird sit on eggs that are not her own. (*Kitzur Shulchan Aruch*, vol. 5, 191:3.)

8. Rejoicing cannot occur at an animal's expense. Therefore, the blessing *shehecheyanu*, thanking God for allowing us to reach a special occasion, and the greeting of *titchadesh* ('may you be renewed in your garment') are not recited when a person first wears leather shoes or furs, because this enjoyment cost an animal's life. (Code of Jewish Law, Orach Chayyim 223:6.)

9. There are probably no creatures that require more the protective divine word against the presumption of people than the animals which, like human beings, have sensations and instincts, but whose body and power are never-

theless subservient to people. In relation to them, human beings so easily forget that injured animal muscle twitches just like human muscle, that the maltreated nerves of an animal sicken like human nerves, that the animal being is just as sensitive to cuts, blows, and beating as people. Thus the human being becomes the torturer of the animal soul, which has been subjected to him only for the fulfillment of humane and wise purposes. Sometimes out of self-interest, at other times in order to satisfy a whim, sometimes out of thoughtlessness—yes, even for the satisfaction of crude satanic desire.

Here you are faced with God's teaching, which obliges you not only to refrain from inflicting unnecessary pain on any animal, but to help and, when you can, to lesson the pain whenever you see an animal suffering, even through no fault of yours.

10. The following Talmudic statement asserts the condemnation of bullfighting: "One who sits in a stadium spills blood." (Talmud Avodah Zarah 1.)

11. A person is not permitted to buy cattle, beast, or bird unless that person can provide adequate food. (Talmud Yevamot 15.)

12. Animals are not to be penned up in stables on Shabbat. (Mechilta to Exod. 23:12.)

13. One who prevents an animal from eating when at work is punishable by flagellation. (*Kitzur Shulchan Aruch*, 186:1.)

14. When horses, drawing a cart, come to a rough road or to a steep hill, and it is hard for them to draw the cart without help, it is our duty to help them, even when they belong to a non-Jew, because of the precept not to be cruel to animals, lest the owner smite them to force them to draw more than their strength permits. (*Kitzur Shulchan Aruch*, 186:2.)

The general principle that emerges from all of these Judaic teachings is that animals may be used for man's benefit, but that the pain caused to the animal must be reduced to the minimum. Also, if the pain is excessive and the benefit to man is one he can well do without, it is better not to use animals even when man does benefit. Thus, things that are permitted according to the strict letter of Jewish law should be avoided if cruelty is excessive. This means that to some extent the law has to be interpreted in such a way that people must decide for themselves to what extent practices involving cruelty to animals should be accepted or rejected, the test being always whether the cruelty is excessive and whether the benefit to humans justifies the act.

Animals
in Liturgy

References to animals by and large do not appear with great frequency in the prayerbook. They do appear in the Sabbath Additional Musaf service, where the reference is to the ancient Sabbath offering: "And on the Sabbath day two he-lambs of the first year without blemish . . ." (Num. 28:9–10). They also appear in the Additional Musaf Festival service with references to the ancient animal sacrifices that were brought in on Jewish festivals. For example, on Passover we call this offering: " . . . you shall present two young bullocks and one ram, and seven he-lambs the first year" (Num. 28:19).

In addition to these two references there are quite a number of references to animals in the prayerbook found in various psalms and in the Five Books of Moses that have been included for liturgical use. Here are several examples:

1. Mountains leaped like rams, and hills like lambs. (Ps. 114:5), recited as part of the Hallel service)

2. Though they surrounded me like bees, they were snuffed out like burning thorns. (Ps. 118:12), recited as part of the Hallel service)

3. For all the glory that they cherish, mortals die, as the beasts that perish. (Ps. 49:21, recited as a psalm of mourning)

4. God gives to the beasts their food, and to ravens that for which they call. (Ps. 147:9)

5. Praise the Lord, O you who are on earth, all sea monsters and ocean depths. (Ps. 148:7)

6. I will sing to God, mighty in majestic triumph, horse and driver God has hurled in the sea. (Exod. 15:1, called the Song of Moses)

7. Human preeminence over beasts is an illusion when all is seen as futility. (excerpted from "Ribon Kol Olameem," a prayer in preliminary morning service)

8. The trees of God drink their fill, the cedars of Lebanon which God planted. Birds build their nests in them; storks have their homes in the pines. (Ps. 104:16)

9. The lions roar for prey, seeking their food from God. (Ps. 1014:21)

There is also a wonderful liturgical response, in the form of a special blessing related to one's sense of wonder and mystery of God's creations. According to the Talmud Berachot 58b, our rabbis have taught that "one who beholds an elephant or an ape says: 'Blessed be You . . . who varies the forms of Your creatures.'"

Perhaps the animal liturgical poem par excellence is that of Chad Gadya—'One Kid'—a song that appears at the end of most Passover Haggadot. Intended for the entertainment of the children to keep them awake until the conclusion of the seder service, the poem consists of ten stanzas written in a nursery rhyme and phrased in the simplest style of Aramaic Hebrew. It was not made part of the actual Haggadah text until late in the sixteenth century, when it was included in the Prague edition of 1590.

The principle idea conveyed in the song is, it seems, identical with Hillel's famous utterance concerning measure for measure: "Because you have drowned others, others have drowned you; and those who have drowned you shall themselves be drowned" (Pirkei Avot 2:7).

Chad Gadya is usually interpreted as an allegory describing the trials and tribulations of Israel's journey through history. In the following theory, each object symbolizes one of Israel's enemies through the years. Israel (the only kid) is purchased by the father (Adonai) for two zuzim (two tablets of the Law) and is subjected to people who supplant each other as Israel's foes: Assyria (cat), Babylon (dog), Persia (stick), Greece (fire), Rome (water), Saracens (ox), the Crusaders (slaughterer), and the Ottomans (angel of death). But in the end the Holy Blessed One saves the Jewish people.

Following is the actual last verse of the song in translation:

"Then came the Holy Blessed One, and slew the angel of death, that killed the slaughterer, that slaughtered the ox, that drank the water that quenched the fire, that burned the stick that beat the dog that bit the cat that ate the goat that father bought for two zuzim. One little goat, one little goat."

Animals in Dreams, Magic, and Omens

Animals were often used to effect magical cures. Although the Bible denied the possibility of magic being an independent power, under certain conditions its use was allowed. In addition, the appearance of certain animals in dreams were considered prognosticators of future events. The following is a cross section of animals and their significance as related to Jewish folklore.

ANIMALS APPEARING IN DREAMS

The following animal appearances in dreams are found in the Talmudic tractate of Berachot 56b–57b:

1. He who sees a bird in his dream should rise early and say, "As birds hovering, so will

the Lord of Hosts protect" [Isa. 31:5], before another sort of verse, such as "Like a sparrow wandering from its nest, so is a person that wanders from his place." [Prov. 27:8]

2. One who sees a cock in his dream may expect a male child. If a hen, a fine garden and joy.

3. There are three sayings in connection with an ox in a dream. If one dreams that he eats of his flesh, he will become rich; if that an ox has gored him, he will have sons that will contend together in the study of Torah; if that an ox bit him, sufferings will come upon him.

4. If one sees a donkey in a dream, one may hope for salvation.

5. If one sees a white horse in a dream, whether walking gently or galloping, it is a good sign. If a red horse, if walking gently it is a good sign. If galloping, it is a bad sign.

6. If one sees a camel in his dream, death has been decreed upon him by Heaven and he has been delivered from it.

7. If one sees an elephant in a dream, a miracle will be wrought for him. If several elephants, wonders of wonders will be wrought for him. The elephants are a good sign if saddled, but a bad omen if not saddled.

8. If one sees a goat in his dream, he will

have a blessed year. If several goats, several blessed years.

9. If one sees a goose in a dream, then he may hope for wisdom. He who dreams of being with one will be head of an academy.

10. If one sees a serpent in a dream, it means that his living is assured. If it bites him, it means that it will be doubled. If he kills it, he will lose his sustenance.

11. All kinds of beasts are a good sign in a dream, except the elephant, monkey, and long-tailed ape.

12. All kinds of birds are a good sign in a dream, except the owl, the horned owl, and the bat.

ANIMALS IN SORCERY AND OPTICAL ILLUSIONS

1. Our Masters taught: A *menachesh* is a diviner who announces, "So-and-so's bread has fallen out of his mouth," "His staff has fallen from his hand," "So and so has called him from behind," "A raven has screamed at him," "A dog has barked at him," "A deer has crossed his path," "A snake has passed at his right and a fox at his left." (Talmud Sanhedrin 65b)

2. Rabbi Eleazar said; "A demon cannot create a creature smaller than a barleycorn." Rabbi Papa said: "By God. Even a creature as large as a camel he cannot create." (Talmud Sanhedrin 67b)

3. Zeiri happened to go to Alexandria in Egypt, where he bought a donkey. When he was about to give it water, it was released from its spell and turned back into a landing bridge. The vendors then said to him, "If you were not Zeiri, we would not return your money to you. Does anyone buy anything without first testing it by water?"

Yannai came to an inn and said: "Give me a drink of water"; a woman offered him a drink of barley flour and honey. When he noticed that her lips were moving, he spilled a little of it, and it turned into scorpions. He said: "As I have drunk of yours, now you drink of mine." So he gave her to drink and she turned into a she-ass. He mounted her and rode to the marketplace. There her friend came and undid the spell and Yannai was thus seen riding upon a woman in public. (Talmud Sanhedrin 67b)

4. Rabbi Yannai said; "I was once walking in the marketplace of Sepphoris where I saw a heretic take a pebble and toss it upward, and when it came down, it had turned into a calf. But did not Rabbi Eleazer say in the name of

Yose bar Zimra, 'If all the world's people assembled, they could not create a single gnat and cast the breath of life into it'? What really happened was that the heretic called to a trickster, who stole a calf from the flock and secretly brought it to him." (Jerusalem Talmud Sanhedrin 7:13)

5. Rav said to Rabbi Chiyya: "I saw an Arab take a sword and cut up his camel. Thus he struck a tabor and the camel stood up whole." Rabbi Chiyya asked Rav, "Was there any blood or dung?" Rav: "No." Rabbi Chiyya: "Since there was not, it must have been an optical illusion." (Talmud Sanhedrin 67b)

ANIMAL CHARMS AND HEALING

1. Our masters taught: The following three are not to pass between two men, nor is one to pass between any two of them: a dog, a date palm, and a woman. Some also say a pig. Some say, also a snake. If one did go between them, what is the remedy? Rabbi Papa said: He should recite the two verses that begin with *El* and end with *El*, [Num. 23:19 and 23:23] or he should begin with a verse that starts with *lo*

["not"] and ends with a verse that also starts with *lo*. (Talmud Pesachim 111a)

2. Those things adversely affect a person's capacity to learn: passing under a camel's bit and all the more so under a camel itself—passing between two camels. (Talmud Horayot 13b)

3. On the Sabbath one may go out carrying a cricket's egg, a fox's tooth, or a nail from the gallows of an impaled convict as a means of healing . . . On the Sabbath one may go out carrying a cricket's egg to cure an ear discharge, a fox's tooth to cure sleep disorders, a live fox's tooth for excessive sleepiness, a dead fox's tooth for sleeplessness. (Talmud Shabbat 67a)

4. Rabbi Huna said: "As a remedy for tertian fever, one should procure seven prickles from seven date palms, seven chips from seven beams, seven pegs from seven bridges, seven handfuls of ash from seven ovens, seven pinches of earth from seven graves, seven bits of pitch from seven ships, seven seeds of cumin, and seven hairs from the beard of an old dog, and tie them inside the collar of one's shirt with a band of twined strands of wool." (Talmud Shabbat 67a)

5. For the demon of the privy one should say, "On the head of a lion and on the snout of a

lioness did we find the demon Bar Shirikai Pandai; with a bed of leeks I felled him, and with the jawbone of an ass I smote him. (Talmud Shabbat 67a)

6. Abbaye said: "My mother told me that the remedy for a fever on the first day is to drink a small pitcher of water. If the fever lasts two days, to let blood. If three days, to eat red meat broiled over coals and drink diluted wine. For continuing fever, a person should get a black hen, tear it lengthwise and crosswise, shave the middle of his head, put the hen on his head, and leave it there until it sticks fast. Then he should go down to the river and stand in the water up to his neck until he is quite faint, and then he should take a dip and come up." (Talmud Gittin 67b)

7. For a migraine, a person should take woodcock and cut its throat with a white silver coin over the side of the head where the pain is concentrated, taking care that the blood does not blind his eyes. Then he should hang the bird on his doorpost, so that he can rub against it when he comes in and when he goes out. (Talmud Gittin 69a)

8. For a cataract a person should take a seven-hued scorpion, dry it out in the shade, and mix two parts of ground kohl to one part of ground scorpion. Then with a paintbrush, ap-

ply three drops to each eye, no more lest the eye burst. (Talmud Gittin 69a)

9. For night blindness, one should take a rope made of wool and with it tie one of his own legs to the leg of a dog, and children should rattle potsherds behind him saying, "Old dog, stupid cock." He should collect seven pieces of raw meat from seven houses, place them in a door socket, and then have the dog eat them over the ash pit of the town. After that, he should untie the rope and people should say to him, "Blindness of so-and-so, son of so-and-so, let go of so-and-so and son of so-and-so, and instead seize the pupils of the dog's eyes."

For day blindness a person should take seven milts from the insides of animals and roast them over a bloodletter's shard. While the blind person sits inside the house, another person should sit outside, and the blind person should say to him, "Give me something to eat." The sighted person should reply, "Take and eat." After the blind person has eaten, he should break the shard. Otherwise, the blindness will come back. (Talmud Gittin 69a)

10. For swelling of the spleen, [one] should take the spleen of a she-goat that has not yet had young, put it inside an oven, stand by it, and say, "As this spleen has dried up, so may

the spleen of so-and-so son of so-and-so, dry up." (Talmud Gittin 69b)

11. Abbaye said: "My mother told me: One who suffers from weakness of the heart should get meat from the right leg of a ram and dried cattle excrement dropped during the month of Nisan." (Talmud Eruvin 29b)

12. Abaye said: "My mother told me: A six-year-old child stung on his birthday by a scorpion is not likely to live. What is a possible remedy? The gall of a white stork in beer. This is to be rubbed into the wound, and the rest should be given to the child to drink." (Talmud Ketubot 50a)

13. Rabbi Abbahu had an earache. So Rabbi Yochanan, so say the sages in the house of study, instructed him: he should take the kidney of a hairless goat, cut it crosswise and lengthwise, put it over glowing coals, and pour the water that comes out of it—neither hot nor cold, but tepid, into the ear. If this remedy does not work, he should take the fat of a large scarab beetle, melt it, and let it drip into the ear. (Talmud Avodah Zarah 28a)

14. When Rabbi Yochanan suffered from scurvy, he went to a Roman noblewoman, who prepared something for him on Thursday and Friday. What did she prepare for him? Rabbi Acha son of Rabbi Ammi said: the water of

leaven, olive oil, and salt. Rabbi Yemar said: leaven itself, olive oil, and salt. Rabbi Ashi said: the fat of goose together with its wing. (Talmud Yoma 84a)

15. One attacked by jaundice should be fed the flesh of a donkey. One bitten by a mad dog should be fed the lobe of its liver. (Talmud Yoma 84a)

16. What causes a dog to go mad? Because women given to witchery have sported with it: thus said Rav. Because an evil spirit rested on it: so said Samuel. What is the difference between the two opinions? If the dog's madness is because an evil spirit rested on it, the dog must be killed by something thrown at him.

We have been taught that Samuel's opinion is right: when the dog is killed, he should be killed only at a distance, with something thrown at him. One against whom a mad dog rubs itself is in danger. One whom it bites will die.

"One against whom a mad dog rubs itself is in danger." What is the remedy? He should remove his garments and run. Once, in the marketplace, a mad dog rubbed itself against Rabbi Huna son of Rabbi Joshua. Rabbi Huna removed his garments and ran, saying: "I applied to myself 'wisdom preserves the life of him who has it.'" (Eccles. 7:12)

"One whom such a dog bites will die." What

is the remedy? Abbaye said: "He should take the skin of a male hyena and write on it, so-and-so, the son of so-and-so, have written against you on the skin of a male hyena: "Kanti, kanti, kleros [some say, Kandi, kandi, kloros]. God, God, Lord of Hosts, Amen, Amen, Selah." Then he should remove his garments and bury them in a cemetery for twelve months. After that, he should take them out, burn them in an oven, and scatter their ashes at a crossroads. (Talmud Yoma 83b–84a)

17. As a remedy for worms in the bowels, pennyroyal should be eaten. With what should it be eaten? With seven black dates. What causes worms in the bowels? Raw meat and water on an empty stomach, fat meat on an empty stomach, ox meat on an empty stomach, nuts on an empty stomach, or shoots of fenugreek eaten on an empty stomach and washed down with water. (Talmud Shabbat 109b)

18. One who is bitten by a snake should procure the embryo of a white she-ass, tear it open, and put it over him; provided however, that the ass was not found to be suffering from a serious organic disease. A certain officer of Pumbedita was bitten by a snake. Now, there were thirteen white she-asses in Pumbedita; all were torn open, and each was found to be suffering from a serious organic disease. There

was another she-ass on the outskirts of the city, but before they could go and bring it, a lion devoured it. Then Abbaye suggested, "Perhaps he was bitten by 'the snake of the sages,' for which there is no cure."

The people replied, "This is so, our master, for when Rav died, Rabbi Isaac bar Bisna decreed that in token of mourning, myrtles and palm branches should not be brought to a wedding feast to the sound of bells, yet this officer did go and bring myrtles and palm branches to a wedding feast to the sound of bells." So a snake bit him, and he died. (Talmud Shabbat 109b)

19. One who has a meatbone stuck in his throat should bring more of that kind of meat, place it on his head, and say, "One by one, go down, swallow; swallow, go down, one by one." (Talmud Shabbat 67a)

ANIMALS AS OMENS

1. If a snake falls upon a bed and one says that the owner of the bed, who is poor, will become rich, or that the pregnant woman will bear a child, or that the maiden will marry a

distinguished man—such auguries are the ways of the Amorites. (Tosafot Shabbat 7)

2. He who wishes to engage in business and wants to ascertain whether he will succeed or not should rear a cock. If it grows plump and handsome, he will succeed. (Talmud Horayot 12a)

3. Our masters taught: When dogs howl, the angel of death has come to the city. When dogs frolic, the prophet Elijah has come to the city. This is so, however, only when there is no bitch among the dogs. (Talmud Baba Kamma 60b)

Proverbs, Parables, and Practical Observations about Animals

Animals have always played a prominent role in Jewish thought. They have been used in proverbs, parables, and sayings. Following is a cross section of noteworthy parables, proverbs, sayings, and practical observations related to the animal kingdom.

PROVERBS

Ant

1. Go the ant, you sluggard, consider her ways and be wise. (Prov. 6:6)
2. The ants are not a mighty people, yet they make ready their food in the summer. (Prov. 30:25)
3. Had not the Torah been given, the ant

would have taught us how to steal. (Talmud Eruvin 100)

4. How wretched is the person who must learn from the ant. (Sifre, Haazinu)

Ass

1. A whip for the horse, a bridle for the ass. (Prov. 26:3)

2. A man follows his donkey after all. (Talmud Baba Metzia)

3. The pace of an ass matches the oats that it eats. (Talmud Shabbat 51)

4. The ass enjoys its hee-haw as much as the nightingale its own sweet notes. (Joseph Caspi, commentary to Prov. 23:16)

5. An ass laden with gold will still munch thistles. (Bikkruei Ha'ittim)

6. An ass feels cold even in the summer solstice. (Talmud Shabbat 53a)

Bear

1. When there is no forest there can be no bears. (Talmud Sotah 47a)

2. When a person enters a town and is accosted by a tax collector, it is as though he had met a bear. (Talmud Sanhedrin 98b)

Bee

1. As the bee gathers for its owner, so Israelites amass merits and good deeds for the glory of the Father in Heaven. (Deut. Rabbah 1)

2. They tell the bee: None of your honey, none of your sting. (Num. Rabbah 20)

3. The bee's honey is sweet and its sting bitter; the honey for its owner, the sting for the rest. (Deut. Rabbah 1)

Bird

1. Better one bird in your cage than a hundred on the wing. (Eccles. Rabbah 4)

2. You see my food but not my cage. (Eccles. Rabbah 11)

Camel

1. As the camel, so the load. (Talmud Ketubot 67)

2. The camel went to get horns, and had its ears cut off instead. (Talmud Sanhedrin 106)

3. The camel does not see its own hump. (Ladino saying)

Cat

1. You don't put the cat in charge of the cream. (Yiddish folk saying)
2. If the Law had not been given to us, we might have learned chastity from the cat. (Talmud Eruvin 100)
3. A sleeping cat does not catch the rat. (Ibn Ezra)

Dog

1. As a dog that returns to its vomit, so is a fool that repeats his folly. (Prov. 26:11)
2. Two dogs in a kennel snarl at each other, but when a wolf comes along they become allies. (Talmud Sanhedrin 105a)
3. One who is bitten by a dog will tremble at its bite. (Zohar, Exod. 45a)
4. You cannot make a dog into a lion. (Deut. Rabbah 3)
5. When one dog barks, all bark together, and to no purpose. (Exod. Rabbah 31)
6. One should not rear a vicious dog in one's home. (Talmud Ketubot 41)
7. Better a live dog than a dead lion. (Eccles. 9:4)
8. A dog when hungry is ready to swallow its own excrement. (Talmud Baba Kamma 92b)

9. If the dog barks enter, if a bitch, leave. (Talmud Eruvin 86a)

10. Five things are said of a mad dog: its mouth is open, its saliva dries, its ears flap, its tail hangs between its legs, and it walks on the edge of roads. Some say: It also barks, but is not heard. (Talmud Yoma 83b)

11. There are three insolent ones: Israel among the nations, the dog among beasts, and the cock among fowls. (Talmud Baba Metzia 25a)

Eagle

1. Though you soar aloft like the eagle and set your nest among the stars, then I bring you down, says God. (Obad. 1:4)

2. The king of birds is the eagle. (Talmud Chagigah 13)

3. If the eagle goes walking, he will be trodden on like any worm. (S. Ben Zion)

Elephant

1. The elephant is frightened of the gnat. (Talmud Shabbat 77)

2. A man is never shown in a dream a golden date palm or an elephant entering the eye of a

needle because he never thinks of such things. (Talmud Berachot 55b)

Fish

1. The big fish in the sea gobble up the little ones. (Talmud Avodah Zarah 4a)
2. One who eats a stinking fish pays dear for it. (Mechilta, Beshallach)
3. Fish are sometimes swallowed by other fish, and sometimes swallow other fish themselves. (Esther Rabbah 7)
4. There are three who gather strength as they get older: a fish, a snake, and a pig. (Talmud Shabbat 77b)

Fly

1. Do not behave to your friend like a fly that quits a healthy spot and settles on a wound. (Eliezer HaGadol, Orchot Chayim)
2. The fly does not kill, but it does spoil. (Ladino saying)
3. [I] never saw a fly pass by his table. (Talmud Berachot 10b)
4. The evil inclination resembles the fly. (Talmud Berachot 61a)

Fox

1. No fox is killed by the earth of his own run. (Jerusalem Talmud Ketubot 83)
2. When a fox has his day, curtsey to him. (Talmud Megillah 16)
3. A fox does not die from the dust of its den. (Talmud Ketubot 71b)
4. Be a tail to lions and not a head to foxes. (Pirkei Avot 4:20)

Goat

1. Black goat's milk and white goat's milk have but one taste. (Gen. Rabbah 87:5)
2. The kids you have left behind have grown to be goats. (Talmud Berachot 63a)

Horse

1. Woe to those who go down to Egypt for help and trust in horses. (Isa. 21:1)
2. A horse is a vain hope for victory. (Ps. 33:17)
3. A whip for the horse, a bridle for the donkey. (Prov. 26:3)
4. Drive your horse with oats, not with a whip. (Yiddish folk saying)
5. Six things are said of a horse: it loves

promiscuity, it loves battle, its spirit is haughty, it despises sleep, it eats much but excretes little, and it walks at the sides of the road. Some say it also wishes to slay its master in battle. (Talmud Pesachim 113b)

Lion

1. The wolf shall dwell with the lamb, and the leopard lie down with the kid . . . and the lion eat straw like the ox. (Isa. 11:6–7)

2. The lion has roared, who will not fear. (Amos 3:8)

3. Better be a tail to a lion than head to a fox. (Pirkei Avot 4:20)

4. The lion you spoke of turns out to be a fox. (Talmud Baba Kamma 117)

5. A scrap will not satisfy the lion. (Talmud Sanhedrin 16)

6. The lion dreads the gnat. (Talmud Shabbat 77)

7. Can a lion become a dog? (Ruth Rabbah 3)

8. A handful does not satisfy the lion's hunger. (Talmud Berachot 50b)

Monkey

1. Men's faces were made to be apelike. (Gen. Rabbah 23)

2. Compared with Sarah, all other people are like a monkey to a human being. (Talmud, Baba Batra 58a)

Mouse

1. A man was nicknamed "the mouse lying on the denarii" [i.e., a miser]. (Talmud Sanhedrin 29b)

2. It is not the mouse that is the thief, it is the hole. If there were no mouse, how should the hole come by? (Talmud Gittin 45a)

3. The cheese and the mouse, which pays the call on the other? (Yalkut Kohelet)

4. Can the mouse be on safe deposit with the cat? (Abarbanel, 1 Sam.)

Ox

1. When an ox falls, many people sharpen their knives. (Talmud Shabbat 32a)

2. You cannot grow two skins off of one ox. (Yiddish folk saying)

3. According to the size of the ox is the feast. As you call Esau great, so will his punishment be. (Gen. Rabbah 65)

4. The ox knows its owner and the donkey its master's crib. (Isa. 1:3)

5. Even when the ox's head is in the feeding

bag, climb up on the roof and throw away the ladder from under you. (Talmud Pesachim 112b)

6. Rabbi Yochanan said: "The best of cattle is the ox, the best of fowls is the chicken." (Talmud Baba Metzia 86b)

Pig

1. If a man drinks properly he becomes strong as a lion, whom nothing in the world can withstand. When he drinks to excess, he becomes like a pig that wallows in mud. (Tanchuma Noah 13:21b)

2. The pig said to the clean animals: "You should be thankful to us because if we were not here it would not be known that you are clean." (Talmud Temurah 2)

3. There is nothing poorer than a dog or richer than a pig. (Talmud Shabbat 155)

4. The pig sticks out its cloven hooves and says: "See, I am clean." (Gen. Rabbah 75)

5. Give a pig a soft branch to eat and he will still grub in the dirt. (Talmud Berachot 43)

6. You cannot make a Sabbath hat out of a pig's tail. (Shalom Aleichem)

7. Hang the heart of a palm on a pig and he will do his usual thing with it. (Talmud Shabbat 155b)

Sheep

1. If no vineyard, why a fence; if no sheep, why a shepherd. (Mechilta, Exod. 12:1)
2. Great is the sheep [i.e., Israel] that lives among seventy wolves [i.e., nations]. (Tanchuma Toldedot 5)
3. Between the careless shepherd and the wolf, the sheep is lost. (Tanchuma Vaera)
4. Whoever behaves as a sheep is devoured by the wolf. (Mincha Chadasha 4:2)

Snake

1. No one can live with a serpent in the same basket. (Talmud Ketubot 72a)
2. A snake may eat the finest delicacies in the world but it still tastes like dust. (Talmud Yoma 75)
3. A snake was asked: "What good do you get of your bite?" It answered: "Instead of asking me, why do you not ask backbiters?" (Deut. Rabbah 5:10)
4. If you are bitten by a snake, you will shy at a rope. (Eccles. Rabbah 7:4)
5. Even with the best of snakes, you had better stamp on its head. (Mechilta, Beshallach)
6. Even concerning snakes, scorpions, spi-

ders, and insects that seem to injure the world, it is written: "It is very good." (Zohar iii, 107)

Wolf

1. The attack by one wolf is not considered an accident that relieves it from responsibility. (Talmud Baba Metzia 93b)
2. That is the way of the world: wolves kill sheep. (Talmud Baba Batra 16)
3. The wolf changes its fur but not its nature. (Mivchar Hapeninim)
4. If a wolf comes to kill you, you are not bound to pat its back. (S.Y. Agnon)
5. In the world to come, the wolf will spin silk and the dog will open gates. (Eccles. Rabbah 1)

Worm

1. The prospects of man are worms. (Pirkei Avot 4:4)
2. A worm is as painful to the dead body as a needle in sound flesh. (Talmud Berachot 18b)
3. Even the moon has no brightness, and the stars are not pure in His sight. How much less man, that is a worm, and the son of man, that is a maggot. (Job 25:6)

PRACTICAL OBSERVATIONS

The following is a cross section of information related to the rabbis' careful observation of and experimentation upon animals. A number of these observations appear quite perceptive by contemporary standards.

1. An unclean fish gives birth to live young, while a clean fish lays eggs. (Talmud Bechorot 7b)

2. Dolphins multiply and increase by coupling like human beings. What are dolphins? Rabbi Judah said: Humans of the sea. (Talmud Bechorot 7b)

3. Whatever animal has its male genital outside gives birth. Whatever has its male genital inside lays eggs. (Talmud Bechorot 7b)

4. All male animals copulate with their faces to the female's back, except three, which copulate face to face—fish, man, and serpents. (Talmud Bechorot 7b)

5. The pig carries its young sixty days after impregnation, and its counterpart among trees is the apple. (Talmud Bechorot 7b)

6. Cattle have a language—each species its own. (Lekach Tov, Gen. 3:1)

7. All fish which have scales have fins. (Mishneh Niddah 6:9)

8. The only mammal which has a cloven hoof but does not chew its cud is the pig. (Talmud Chullin 59a)

9. The lifetime of a fly is less than one year. (Talmud Chullin 58b)

10. Snakes shed their skin periodically, and their venom loses its potency as they age. (Talmud Avodah Zarah 30b)

11. Roosters are able to shatter glass by crowing into it. (Talmud Baba Kamma (18b)

12. The wolf, the lion, the leopard, the panther, the elephant, the tailless ape, and the long-tailed ape carry their young 3 years. (Talmud Bechorot 8a)

PARABLES AND STORIES

Ant

1. Rabbi Simeon ben Chalafta read Proverbs 6:6: "Go to the ant you sluggard; consider her ways and be wise; which having no chief, overseer, or ruler, provides her bread in the summer and gathers her food in the harvest."

By nature the rabbi was fond of discovering things for himself. Knowing that the ants dislike the sun, he went out to a field and spread his mantle over an anthill. A single ant emerged, and the rabbi quickly dashed some paint upon it in order to be able to identify it. The ant ran back and soon returned with a considerable company of ants who apparently expected to find shade. Before this, however, the rabbi had removed his mantle. He saw the group of ants turn against the leader who had lured them out of his promise of shade, and they killed him.

"Had these ants a ruler," thought the rabbi, "he would have instituted judgment and designated an appropriate form of punishment." (Talmud Chullin 57)

Ass

1. Once the ass of Rabbi Chanina ben Dosa was stolen by brigands. They tied it up in a yard and placed before it straw, barley, and water, but it would not drink or eat. They then said: "Why should we allow it to die and befoul our yard?" They opened its gate and drove it away. It walked along the path braying until it reached the home of Rabbi Chanina ben Soda. When it arrived, the rabbi's son heard its voice and said to his father: "This sounds like our beast." The rabbi answered: "My son, open the door, for it is dying of hunger." The son immediately placed before it barley, straw, and wa-

ter. It ate and drank. Thus it was said: "Even as the righteous of old were saintly, so too were the beasts saintly like their masters." (Avot de Rabbi Natan, Chapter 8)

2. A certain person had a filly, a she-ass, and a sow. He measured out fodder to the she-ass and the filly, but let the sow eat as much as she wanted. The filly complained to the she-ass, "What is this idiot doing? To us, who do the work of the master, he rations food, but to the sow, who does nothing, he gives as much as she wants." The she-ass replied, "The time will come when you will see that she is stuffed with fodder not out of deference to her but to her own harm." When the Roman Calends came, they took the sow and struck her. (Esther Rabbah 7:1)

3. Rabbi Yose of Yodkart had a donkey. When hired out for the day, the pay would be sent attached to the donkey's back, and he would bring it back to his master Rabbi Yose. If the amount was too little or too much, the donkey would not move from his place. Once, a pair of sandals were forgotten on the donkey's back, and he refused to budge until they were removed. (Talmud Taanit 24a)

4. While on a journey, Rabbi Pinchas ben Yair came to a certain inn, where some barley was placed before his she-ass, which she re-

fused to eat. It was then mashed up, but still she refused to eat. It was carefully picked, but still she refused to eat. "Perhaps," suggested Rabbi Pinchas, "the barley had not been tithed?" So the barley was tithed, and only then did the she-ass eat it. (Talmud Chullin 7a–b)

5. Rabbi Alexandri said: "Two ass drivers who hated each other were walking on a road when one of [the asses] collapsed under its burden. The other driver saw this but continued on his way. But then he reflected: "Does not the Torah say, 'If you see the ass of one who hates you lying flat under its load and your inclination is to refrain from raising it, you must nevertheless raise it with him' (Exod. 23:5)?" So he returned, lent a hand, and helped his enemy rearrange the load. He began talking to his enemy: "Loosen it a bit here, pull a little tighter there, unload over there." Before long, peace developed between the two of them, so that the driver of the unloaded ass reflected, "I thought he hated me, but look how compassionate he was." By and by, the two entered an inn, ate and drank together, and became friends. What caused them to make peace and become friends? Because one of them kept what was written in the Torah. Hence, "You have estab-

lished harmony." [Ps. 99:4]. (Tanchuma, Mishpatim 1)

Bird

1. A bird made its nest at the edge of the sea, only to have it swept away when the tide rose. What did the bird do? It proceeded to take into its beak water from the sea and pour it out on the dry land, then take sand from the dry land and drop it into the sea. His friend stopped to watch, and then asked, "What are you doing, wearing yourself out like this?" The bird answered, "I will not budge from here until I turn the sea into dry land and the dry land into sea." His friend said, "You are the biggest fool in the world. After all of this effort, what do you think that you can accomplish?" (Esther Rabbah 7:10)

2. A bird was confined to a cage. Another bird flew up, perched above the caged one, and said, "How happy you must be that your food is provided for you." The bird in the cage responded, "Bad luck to you. All you see is the food. You don't see the bars on the cage." (Eccles. Rabbah 11:9)

3. A bird hunter caught a bird and was about to catch a second when that bird perched itself on a king's statue. At this, the hunter stood still,

perplexed, and said to himself: "If I throw stones at her, I will forfeit my life, and if I try poking at her with my stick, I am afraid I might strike the king's image. I don't know what to say to you, except that you fled to a perfect place and made good your escape." (Exod. Rabbah 27:6)

4. Rabbi Ilish was taken captive, together with a man who understood the language of birds. When a raven came by and crowed, Rabbi Ilish asked the man, "What does it say?" The man replied, "It says 'Ilish, Ilish, flee.'" So Rabbi Ilish said, "The raven is a liar, and one should not rely on it."

Then a dove came along and called. Rabbi Ilish again asked the man, "What does it say?" The man replied, "Ilish, flee. Ilish, flee." Rabbi Ilish said: "Since the congregation of Israel is likened to a dove, I am being told that a miracle will be wrought for me." So both men made a break for it. A miracle was performed for Rabbi Ilish and he got safely across the bridge but the man with Rabbi Ilish was caught and put to death. (Talmud Gittin 54a)

5. Rabbi Simeon ben Chalafta was an observer of nature. Now, in his orchard, he had a tree trunk, and he saw a hoopoe building its nest in it. So, saying to himself: "What business does this unclean bird have in my orchard?"

Rabbi Simeon ben Chalafta proceeded to demolish the nest. The hoopoe went and repaired it. What did Rabbi Simeon ben Chalafta then do? He brought a board, placed it at the opening of the nest, and made it stay put by driving a nail into it. What did the hoopoe do? It brought a certain herb, placed it on the nail, and pulled it out. Rabbi Simeon ben Chalafta decided: "It would be a good idea if I were to hide this herb, so that thieves may not learn to do likewise and bring humankind to ruin." (Lev. Rabbah 22:4)

6. The rabbis said: the raven is cruel. When it begets fledglings and sees that they are white while he is black, he abandons them and goes away. Then the Holy One provides a sustenance for them.

Rabbi Assi was an observer of nature. When he once saw a raven building its nest, laying eggs, and hatching fledglings, he took the fledglings and put them in a new pot, whose top he sealed with plaster. After three days, he opened the top, found out what the fledglings were doing, and found that their droppings had produced gnats, which the fledglings ate as they flew up. Rabbi Assi applied to them the verse "Who provides for the raven his prey." (Job 38:41)

7. In the days of Rabbi Chiyya Rabbah a new

bird came to Palestine. By reason of the sound of its chirp it was called *zarzir*. Rabbi Chiyya was asked if it was permitted to use this bird as food. He said: "Watch the sort of bird we know, with which it associates."

It was found that the Egyptian crow kept company with the zarzir on the roofs of the town. Thereupon Rabbi Chiyya pronounced the zarzir unclean. Then the saying was born: For good reason the crow went to the zarzir: because they belonged to the same species. (Gen. Rabbah 65)

8. A heron used to sing in the house of his master. While he sat and dined, the heron would sing. Presently the master brought a young hawk into the house. When the heron saw it, he fled under the bed, hid himself, and would no longer open his mouth. The master came in to dine and asked a member of his household, "Why doesn't the heron sing?" He was told, "Because you brought a young hawk in on him, he has ceased to sing out of fear. Remove the young hawk, and the heron will sing again." (Aggadat Bereshit 58)

Dog

1. Rabbi Tanchum bar Maryon said: "I observed in Rome some dogs with human sagac-

ity. When one of them became hungry, he lay down on the ground before a baker's shop, and pretended to sleep. As soon as the baker began to slumber, the dog overturned the bread on the floor of the shop. Before the baker had time to pick it up, the dog had run away with a loaf. It is in these devious ways that Satan labors to compel a person to sin." (Gen. Rabbah 22)

2. Two dogs tending a flock were always quarreling. When the wolf attacked one, however, the other thought: "If I do not help my neighbor today, the wolf may attack me tomorrow."

Thereupon the two dogs settled their differences, and together they killed the wolf. (Talmud Sanhedrin 105a)

Ewe

1. On the Sabbath ewes may not go out protected in a certain way [Talmud Shabbat 5:4]. "'Protected' here means," said Rabbi Acha bar Ulla while seated before Rabbi Chisda, "that after a ewe is shorn, a compress saturated with oil is placed on her forehead, so that she will not catch cold." Rabbi Chisda replied, "If so, you would treat a ewe as though she were Mar Ukba." But Rabbi Papa bar Samuel, while seated before Rabbi Nachman, said, "'Protected' means that when a ewe is about to

kneel for lambing, two compresses saturated with oil are made for her, one placed on her forehead, and the other over her womb, so that she may keep warm." Rabbi Nachman replied: "If so, you would treat a ewe as though she were Yalta" [wife of Rabbi Nachman]. Finally, to explain 'protected', Rabbi Huna said: "There is a certain wood in cities far across the sea called *hanun,* a chip of which is brought and placed in the ewe's nostril to make her sneeze and thus expel the worms inside her head." (Talmud Shabbat 54b)

2. There was a ewe in our neighborhood in whose windpipe there was a hole, and when a tube of reed was fitted into it, the ewe recovered. (Talmud Chullin 57b)

Fish

1. Rabbi Safra related: "Once, while traveling on a ship, we saw a fish that raised its head out of the sea. It had horns on which were engraved: 'I, one of the lesser creatures of the sea, am 300 parasangs long, and yet I can fit into Leviathan's mouth.'"

Rabbi Ashi said: "This fish was a sea-goat." (Talmud Baba Batra 74a)

2. Rabbi Yochanan related: "Once, while traveling on a ship, we saw a chest set with

precious stones and pearls, and encompassed by a species of fish called karsha. When a diver went down to bring up the chest, a fish attacked him and was about to bite off his thigh. But the diver threw a bottle full of vinegar at it and was able to continue his dive. Just then, a divine voice came forth and said: 'What have you people to do with the chest that belongs to Rabbi Chania ben Dosa's wife, who is to store in it purple dye for the righteous in the world to come.'" (Talmud Baba Batra 74a–b)

3. Rabbah bar Bar Chanah said: "Once, while traveling on a ship, we saw a fish in whose nostrils a stickleback had entered, so that the fish died. When the water cast the dead fish onto the shore, sixty towns were destroyed thereby, sixty towns ate of it, and sixty towns salted what was left of it, and 300 kegs of oil were filled from one of its eyeballs. On returning after twelve months, we saw that the building joints were being sawn from its skeleton, and with these the towns were rebuilt. (Talmud Baba Batra 73a–b)

4. A righteous man was accustomed to honor all Sabbaths and Jewish festivals. Once, on Yom Kippur, he went to the market and found there only one fish for sale. The governor's servant was also there, and bid the other man for the fish. Eventually, the Jew bought it.

At dinner, the governor asked why there was no fish and when he was informed that a Jew had bought it, he accused the Jew of having hidden a treasure belonging to the king.

The Jew pleaded that as Yom Kippur was the Sabbath of Sabbaths that he must honor it by buying that fish. The governor acquitted him, and the Almighty rewarded the Jew and prepared for him a precious jewel in the fish. The Jew was able to live off of the proceeds of the jewel for the rest of his entire life. (Pesikta Rabbati 11a)

Fowl

1. Rabbi Simeon ben Chalafta had a hen that lost her femur. So they provided her with a tube of reed for support, and she recovered. It is said of Rabbi Simeon ben Chalafta, who was an observer of nature, that he did something to disprove Rabbi Judah's view, for Rabbi Judah maintained, "If a bird's down is gone, it is unfit to be eaten." Now Rabbi Simeon ben Chalafta had a hen whose down was entirely gone. So, after first wrapping the hen in a bronze workers' leather apron, he kept her in an oven, and the new down she grew was more abundant than before. (Talmud Chullin 57b)

2. The partridge brings eggs of other birds

and sits on them, until they emerge from their shells as chicks. They then climb on his back, pluck his feathers, and eat them. When the partridge wishes to flee from them, he cannot, because his feathers have been plucked. Then, when a reptile or a beast comes upon him, it eats him. What brought such a fate upon him? The fact that he brooded on eggs that were not his. (Tanchuma Yalkut, Jer. 297)

Fox

1. A fox was walking on a river bank and, seeing schools of fish swimming here and there, asked them, "From whom are you fleeing?" They replied, "From the nets and traps set for us by men." So the fox said to them, "How would you like to come up on dry land, so that you and I could live together, the way my ancestors lived with yours?" They replied, "You, the one they call the most clever of animals, are in fact a fool. If we are fearful in the place where we can stay alive, how much more fearful would we be in a place where we are sure to die." (Talmud Berachot 61b)

2. The fox said to the wolf, "Go into a Jewish courtyard on a Sabbath eve and help them prepare whatever is needed for the meal, and you will eat with them on the Sabbath." But

when the wolf was about to enter, the court-yard's residents banded together against him with clubs.

Then the wolf was set on killing the fox, but the fox said, "They beat you only because of your father, who on one occasion helped them prepare a meal and then devoured every luscious morsel." The wolf: "Should I be beaten up because of my father?" The fox: "Yes— 'Fathers eat sour grapes, and their children's teeth are blunted.' [Ezek. 18:2] But come with me, and I will show you a place where you can eat your fill."

The fox led the wolf to a well. Across the well's mouth was a beam with a rope wound over it. At each end of the rope was tied an empty bucket. The fox climbed into the upper bucket, and his weight caused it to plunge downward, while the lower bucket flew up-ward. The wolf came down to him. "Why did you go down there?" The fox: "Because here there is meat and cheese enough to eat one's fill," and he pointed to the moon's reflection in the water. It looked like a round cheese. The wolf: "How am I to go down?" The fox: "Climb into the upper bucket." The wolf did so, and his weight caused it to plunge down, while the bucket with the fox flew up. The wolf: "How am I to get up again? The fox: "'The righteous is delivered out of his trouble, and the wicked comes in his stead' [Prov. 11:1]. Is it not written, 'Just balances, just weights' [Lev. 19:36]?" (Rashi on Talmud Sanhedrin 39a)

3. A fox found a vineyard that was fenced in on all sides, except for one narrow gap through which he tried to enter but could not. What did he do? He fasted for three days, until he became lean and slender, and thus got through the gap. But then, after he ate his fill of grapes, he became fat again, so that when he tried to leave through the same gap, he could not. He again fasted three days, until he once more became lean and slender. Thus having returned to his former size, he was able to leave. He turned his face back to the vineyard and gazed at it, saying, "O vineyard, vineyard, how good are you, and how good is the fruit within you. All that is within you is beautiful and comely. But what benefit can one derive from you? As one goes into you, so must one come out." (Eccles. Rabbah 5:14)

Gazelle

Rabbi Levi in the name of Rabbi Simeon ben Lakish said: "The gazelle is the animal that is most beloved by God. When she gives birth to a fawn, God sends an herb to heal her. When she is thirsty, she digs her horns into the ground and moans. God hears her plea and she senses out water in the deep pits. When she goes forth to drink, she is at first in terror of the other beasts, but God imbues her with courage. She stamps with her feet and uses her horns. The beasts then flee from her. Why does God love her so much? Because she harms and disturbs the peace of no one." (Midrash 9 Sam.)

Goose

Rabbah bar Chana said: "We were once traveling in the desert and saw geese whose feathers fell out on account of their fatness, and streams of fat flowed under them. I said to them: 'Shall we have a share of your flesh in the world to come?' When I came before Rabbi Eleazer he said to me: 'Israel will be called to account for the sufferings of these geese.'" (Talmud Baba Batra 73b)

Lion

1. In the days of Rabbi Joshua ben Chananiah, the Emperor of Rome issued a decree that the Holy Temple be rebuilt. The Samaritans immediately came forward with the same arguments they had used in the days of Zeruba-

bel. The Emperor's government then issued a decree that the plan must follow the Emperor's measurements, and that the Temple must be built on a new site. The Jews could not consent to this change, and were greatly incensed.

Rabbi Joshua called the people together and said: "A lion while eating found that a bone stuck in his throat. He roared out that whosoever would remove the bone would be rewarded. A stork thrust its long bills into the lion's throat and drew forth the bone. He then asked for the reward. 'Your reward,' said the lion, 'is that you will be able henceforth to boast that you are the only creature whose head was in the lion's mouth and came out alive.' So it is with us—it is enough that we have emerged without harm from a decree by the Emperor." (Gen. Rabbah 64)

2. A lion became angry at all beasts, both wild and tame. So they said: "Who will go and pacify him?" The fox spoke up: "Come with me to him. I know 300 parables with which to pacify him." They replied, "Let's go." After walking a short distance, he stopped. So they asked him, "What is the matter?" The fox: "I forgot a hundred parables." They said: "There is ample power for good in 200." He walked a little farther and stopped again. They again asked: "What is the matter?" The fox replied:

"I forgot another hundred." They then said: "There is ample power for good even in a hundred parables." When they were nearing their destination, he said, "I forgot all of them. Each of you, go and pacify the lion in your own behalf." (Gen. Rabbah 78:7)

3. The lion gave a feast to all animals, wild and tame, and provided a pavilion for them out of lions' skins. After they had eaten and drunk, they said, "Who will write an appropriate verse for our entertainment?" and looked to the fox. He asked, "Will you respond 'Amen' to what I am about to say?" They answered, "Yes." The fox lifted his eyes toward the skins above and said, "May God who has shown us what happened to those above show us what is to happen to the one below." (Esther Rabbah 7:3)

4. Once, Rabbi Chanina ben Dosa saw a lion and said to him: "O you weakling of a king, have I not adjured you not to be seen in the Land of Israel?" The lion fled at once, but Rabbi Chanina ran after him and said: "Forgive me having called you 'weakling,' for God who created you and called you "mighty"—"the lion which is mightiest among the beasts" [Prov. 30:30]. (Tanchuma Vayiggash 3)

5. Rav Papa said: "We have a tradition that a lion will not attack two persons. But we see that it does. However, so Rami Bar Abba ex-

plained, no wild beast will endeavor to over-
power a human being unless he appears to it to
be an animal, as is said, 'Man will not abide in
honor when he appears to be an animal—he
will perish'" [Ps. 49:13]. (Talmud Shabbat 151b)

6. It happened that a lion, a dog, and an
Ethiopian gnat were together. The lion was
about to mangle the dog, but when he saw the
Ethiopian gnat, he drew back in fear, for the
Ethiopian gnat is the scourge of the lion, even
as the dog is the scourge of the Ethiopian gnat.
Thus, the three creatures did no harm to one
another. When Rabbi Akiva saw this, he quoted,
"How manifold are Your works, O God. In wis-
dom have You made them all" [Ps. 104:24).
(Midrash Tehillim 104:19)

Lizard

1. Rabbi Muna bar Torta said: "Once I went
to a place where crossbreeding was practiced,
and I saw a snake wrapped around a lizard.
After some days, an *arod* emerged from between them. When I came with this tale before
Rabbi Simeon the Pious he said to me: 'The
Holy One declares: "These people have been
bringing into being creatures that I did not
create in My world. I too will bring upon them

a much more dangerous creature that I did not create in My world."'" (Talmud Chullin 127a)

2. Our masters taught: In a certain place there was once an *arad* [possibly a cross between a snake and a lizard] who used to injure people. People came and told Rabbi Chanina ben Dosa about this. He said, "Show me its hole." They did so, and he put his heel over the hole. The arod came out, bit him, and immediately died. He hoisted it on his shoulder, brought it to the house of study, and said, "See, my children, it is not the venomous lizard that kills, it is sin that kills."

On that occasion they said: "Woe to the person who meets up with a venomous lizard and woe unto the venomous lizard who meets up with Rabbi Chanina ben Dosa." (Talmud Berachot 33a)

3. When a havarbar lizard stings a man, if the man is the first to get to water, the lizard will die. But if the lizard is the first to get to water, the man will die.

It has been told that while Rabbi Chanina ben Dosa was standing for the *Tefillah* ["prayer"], a havarbar lizard came and stung him, but he did not interrupt his *Tefillah*. Then they went and found that lizard dead at the entrance to his hole. When Rabbi Chanina's students asked him, "Master, did you not feel the sting?" he replied, "May such and such come upon me if I felt anything, my heart being concentrated utterly on the *Tefillah*. (Jerusalem Talmud Berachot 5:1)

Mouse

1. Mice are feral and want to eat everything before their eyes. So when mice see a great deal of produce, they call their comrades to help them eat. (Jerusalem Talmud, Baba Metzia 3:5)

2. Rabbi Eleazar was asked by his students: Why do all people persecute mice? Because of their malicious nature. In what way is it demonstrated? Rava said: "They chew up even clothing." Rabbi Papa said: "They will chew up even the handle of a mattock." (Talmud Horavot 13a)

Salamander

There are creatures that grow in fire but cannot grow in air. Which is one? The salamander. How does it come into being? When makers of glass heat their furnace for seven successive days and seven successive nights, there emerges from the fierceness of the fire a creature resembling a mouse, which people call *salamander*. If a man applies its blood to his hand or to any of his limbs, fire has no power over that spot. Why? Because the salamander's origin is fire. (Tanchuma Vayeshev 3)

Scorpion

1. Samuel saw a scorpion mount a frog, cross a river, bite a man, who then died. Accordingly, he applied to the frog and the scorpion the verse, "They stand this day to carry out Your judgments, for all are Your servants" [Ps. 119:91]. (Talmud Nedarim 41a)

2. The Holy One carries out a mission of His through everything, even through a snake, even through a scorpion, even through a frog, even through a gnat.

Rabbi Chanan of Sepphoris said: "There is the story of a scorpion proceeding to the other side of the Jordan to carry out a mission given to him. The Holy One provided him with a frog, upon whose back he crossed the river. Then, moving on, he stung a man to death. His mission thus completed, the scorpion was brought back to his place by the frog." (Gen. Rabbah 10:7)

Snake

1. A philosopher sought to learn how long a snake requires to bear her offspring. He placed a male and a female snake in a box and cared for them. After seven years a baby snake was born. Proud of his newly acquired knowledge, he accosted Rabbi Gamaliel and Rabbi Joshua. He placed the question before them, and Rabbi Joshua gave the correct answer. The philosopher knocked his head against the wall in chagrin, saying: "It cost me infinite pains for many years to discover what the rabbis have told me offhand." (Gen. Rabbah 20)

2. Rabbi Chalafta said: "The snake loves garlic in any form. Once, a wandering snake crept into a house, attracted by the odor of garlic. The creature ate it and then spat venom into the plate. A pet snake of the household, however, observing this, filled the plate with earth, and thereby saved the life of its master."

Rabbi Meir said: "Once some shepherds milked a cow and placed the crock on the ground. A snake drank from it and spat venom into the crock. The shepherd dog observed this and barked furiously when his masters came to drink the milk. When they paid no attention, he leaped at them and overturned the crock. The venom affected the dog and he died. The shepherds in gratitude placed a monument at his grave telling of his loyalty and martyrdom. (Jerusalem Talmud Terumot 8, 3)

3. Rabbi Acha said: "Rabbi Chiyya the Elder told me the following: 'There was once a man in the Land of Israel who was called Baldhead. Why? Because it is said that he once went up to the top of a mountain to gather wood. There he saw a serpent the size of a beam in an olive press, sound asleep. And even though the serpent did not see him, the man's hair fell out, and no hair grew on him again to the day of his death. Thus he was called Baldhead.'" (Exod. Rabbah 24:4)

4. Rabbi Pinchas told in the name of Rabbi Chanan of Sepphoris the story of a certain man who was reaping and binding sheaves in the valley of Bet Tofet. When the heat of the day came, he took some herbs and made them into a wreath, which he tied to his head. Later, a big snake came to attack him, and he rose up and killed it. A snake charmer passed by, saw the dead snake, fixed his eyes on the man, and said, "I am amazed. Who slew this snake?" The man said: "I killed it." When the snake charmer noticed the herbs made into a wreath on the man's head, he asked him, "Did you really kill this snake?" The man said: "Yes." The snake charmer said: "Would you mind removing the

herbal wreath from your head?" The man answered: "Not at all." The charmer then said: "Would you mind picking up the snake with my staff?" The man said: "Not at all." But as soon as the man drew near to the snake, even before he touched it, he fell to pieces limb by limb. (Gen. Rabbah 10:7)

5. Once, a man was walking in a field holding a jug of milk in his hand. A snake moaning with thirst met him. "Why are you moaning?" asked the man. "Because I am thirsty," replied the snake; "what is that you have in your hand?" The man answered: "Milk." The snake then said: "Give me the milk to drink, and I will show you so much money that you will be rich." The man gave the milk to the snake, and it drank.

After the snake had drunk, the man said: "Show me the money of which you spoke." The snake responded: "Follow me." He followed it until they came to a large stone. The snake then said, "The money is hidden under this stone." The man lifted the stone, dug down, and found the money, which he took and was about to carry to his house.

What did the snake then do? It sprang up and coiled itself around the man's neck. "Why are you doing this?" the man asked. The snake responded: "I am going to kill you because you took all of my money." Said the man: "Come with me to Solomon before his court."

They went and appeared before Solomon, the snake still coiled around the man's neck. The man made his plea to the king.

"What are you after?" the king asked the snake. It answered: "I want to kill him." "Get off his neck," said the king. "Since both of you are in court, it is not right that you should have a hold on him while he has no hold on you." So the snake slithered off of the man's neck to the ground. The king then said: "Now you can have your say." The snake began his plea: "I wish to kill the man, in keeping with what the Holy One said to me: 'You shall strike him in the heel'" [Gen. 3:15]. Then the king said to the man, "And the Holy One commanded you, 'He is to strike you in the head.'" The man immediately sprang forward and smashed its head.

Hence the proverb: "Smash the head of even the best of snakes." (Tanchuma B, Introduction)

6. As Rabbi Yannai was sitting and lecturing at the gate of his town, he saw a snake slithering rapidly toward the town. When it was chased away from one side, it resumed its journey on the other side. When chased away from that side, it kept going forward on the side where it had been first. So Rabbi Yannai said, "This

creature is on its way to carry out a mission."
Soon after, a report spread in the town: "So and
so was bitten by a snake and is dead." (Gen.
Rabbah 10:7)

Snail

1. Our masters taught: The purple snail resembles the sea in its essence. Its shape resembles a fish, it comes up from the sea once in
70 years. The blue thread is dyed with its
blood. It is for this reason that it is so expen-
sive. (Talmud Menachot 44a)

2. Go out into a valley, and you will see a
mouse that today is half-flesh and half-earth,
and tomorrow it will have become a reptile, so
that all of it will be flesh.

Go up to a mountain and you will see that
today there is only one snail, but tomorrow,
after rain comes down, the whole mountain
will be filled with snails. (Talmud Sanhedrin
91a)

Spider

Once, while seated in his garden, David, King
of Israel, saw a wasp eating a spider. David
spoke up to the Holy One: "Master of the Universe, what benefit is there from these two

creatures that You created? The wasp merely despoils the nectar of flowers—no benefit from it. The spider spins all year but makes no clothing." The Holy One replied: "You belittle My creatures. The time will come when you will need both."

Later, while fleeing from King Saul, David took refuge in a cave, and the Holy One sent a spider, which spun a web across the cave's entrance, sealing it. When Saul came and saw the cave's entrance with the web across it, he said, "Surely no person has come in here, for had he done so, he would have torn the web." So Saul went away without going into the cave.

As David left the cave and saw the spider, he blew it a kiss saying, "Blessed be your Creator, and blessed be you."

Subsequently, David found Saul asleep within a barricade, with Abner lying prone across the tent's entrances, his head in one entrance and his feet in the opposite entrance. Abner's knees were raised up, and so David was able to come in under them and pick up the cruse of water. As he was about to leave the way he came, Abner stretched out his legs, which were like two gigantic columns in size, pinning David down. David, beseeching the Holy One's compassion, prayed, "My God, My God, why have You forsaken me?" [Ps. 22:2] At that, the Holy

One performed a miracle for him. God sent him a big wasp, which stung Abner's legs so that he again raised his knees, and thus David was free to leave.

In that instant, David said in praise of the Holy One: "Master of the Universe, who can imitate Your works, Your mighty acts?" [Deut. 3:24]—All Your works are beautiful. (Alphabet of Ben Sira)

The Use of Snails in Biblical Blue Dyes

In ancient times the purple and blue dyes derived from snails were so rare and sought-after that they were literally worth their weight in gold. These precious dyes colored the robes of the kings and princes of Media, Babylon, Egypt, and Greece. To wear them was to be identified with royalty.

Twice daily traditional Jews recite the following passage from Numbers 15:37–39:

God said to Moses: "Speak to the children of Israel and say to them that they shall make for themselves fringes on the corners of their garments throughout their generations. And they shall place upon each fringe a thread of *techelet* ['blue'] . . . And you shall see it and remember all the commandments of God and you shall do them."

This God-given command to affix a thread of blue to the corners of one's garment was meant to be a constant and conspicuous reminder of the Israelites' stature as noble children of the Sovereign of the Universe, constantly pursuing His *mitzvot* ['religious obligations'].

The Mediterranean coast was the center of the dyeing industry in the ancient world. "Tyrian purple" came from the port city of Tyre in Phoenicia (now south Lebanon). Some say that the etymology of the word *Phoenician* itself is that of the color purple.

Because of its lucrative nature, purple dyeing eventually came under imperial control. The Romans issued edicts that only royalty could wear garments colored with these dyes. The oppression apparently drove the Jewish blue-making industry underground, and later, with the Arab conquest of Israel (in 639 c.e.), the secret of *techelet* was essentially lost and the dyeing process obscured.

The biblical commandment to wear fringes on the corner of one's garment is still widely observed today with the donning of a prayershawl, or *tallit*, by Jewish boys of Bar Mitzvah age. In Conservative, Reform, and Reconstructionist settings girls of Bat Mitzvah age may also choose to wear the prayershawl. But the prominent blue thread has all but been forgotten. What has remained are the various passages in the Talmud describing the ancient source of the blue dye—a snail known as the *hilazon*. This creature's most notable features were that it had a shell, it could be found along the northern coast of Israel, and that its body was "similar to the sea." The main characteristic of the dye made from it was that its color was "similar to the sky and sea."

In 1858 the French zoologist Henri de Lacaze-Duthiers found that three mollusks in the Mediterranean sea produced purple-blue dyes. One, the *murex trunculus*, was determined by him (and other scientists) to be the source of the ancient biblical blue.

In the same century Rabbi Gershon Hanoch Leiner set out on an expedition to search for the lost hilazon. He was convinced that a certain type of squid fit the description of the coveted snail. Unable to produce a blue dye from the black ink released by the squid, he turned to an Italian chemist, who provided him with a method. Within 2 years, thousands of Rabbi Leiner's followers were wearing blue threads on their fringes.

In 1913 the Chief Rabbi of Ireland, Rabbi Isaac Herzog (later to become the Chief Rabbi of Israel) wrote a doctoral dissertation on the subject of Hebrew *porphyrology* (the study of purple—a word he coined). When he sent samples of Rabbi Leiner's blue to chemists for analysis, the results were unanimous. The dye was inorganic—a synthetically manufactured color known as Prussian blue. Refusing to believe that Rabbi Leiner had purposely misled his constituents, Rabbi Herzog studied Rabbi Leiner's dyeing process. He discovered the truth, which was that the process called for subjecting the squid ink to intense heat and then adding colorless iron fillings to the mixture. This produced the blue color that indeed appeared to come from the squid ink. The Rabbi had apparently been misled by an unscrupulous chemist.

Rabbi Herzog knew of the work done by Lacaze-Duthiers and others and realized that all the evidence pointed to the murex trunculus as the most likely source for the techelet. The riddle of producing a pure blue color from the snail was accidentally solved. While researching the methods used by the ancient dyers, a professor Otto Isner of the Shekar College of Fibers noticed that on cloudy days, trunculus dye tended towards purple, but on sunny days it was a brilliant blue. Recent archaeological excavations in Tyre uncovered mounds of murex shells dating from biblical times that were broken in the exact spot necessary to obtain the dyestuff.

Today in Israel there is a nonprofit organization called *Amutat P'til Techelet*, comprised of a group who devote their entire time to obtaining the snails that produce the techelet dye, extracting it and dyeing fringes for prayer shawls.

Perek Shira:
Chapter of Song

The volume entitled *Perek Shira: Chapter of Song* is by far one of the most unique and unusual ones in all of Jewish literature. According to some scholars, the book is one of the oldest texts of Merkavah mysticism, the first flowering Jewish mysticism in the early centuries of the Common Era. First mentioned in a polemical work of Salmon ben Jeroham, a tenth-century Jerusalemite, its liturgical use was revived in the mystical city of Safed in the sixteenth century as it began to be recited as a prayer.

Perek Shira is a collection of sayings in praise of God the Creator. What makes the book mysterious and compelling is that the sayings in praise of God have been placed in the mouth of God's creatures. All creation, except humans, is represented—the natural and supernatural

165

orders, inanimate nature, the heavens and their hosts, the world of plants, and the world of animals, each according to its kind. Together the hymns comprise a kind of cosmic song of praise sung by the whole of creation. Most of the hymns are biblical verses, the greater part of them citations from the Book of Psalms.

The following are those excerpts from *Perek Shira* that specifically relate to animals.

THE PREFACE

By the beasts of the earth and the birds of the sky, He makes us wise.

(Job 35:11)

Rabbi Yochanan said: "Even if we have not been given the Torah we still would have learned modesty from the cat, honesty from the ant, chastity from the dove, and good manners from the rooster.

(Talmud Eruvin 100b)

. . . Our rabbis tell the following story: "At the time that King David completed the Book of Psalms, he became full of pride and said to the Holy Blessed One, 'Surely there is no creature which You have made that can sing songs and praises greater than mine.'

"At that exact moment a frog appeared before him and said, 'David, do not be so proud, for I can sing songs and praises even greater than yours. And not only that, but in every song that I sing there exist three thousand allegories. For it is said: "He composed three thousand proverbs, and his songs numbered one thousand and five."'" (1 Kings 5:12)

THE SONGS

. . . The rooster says: "At the time that the Holy Blessed One comes among the righteous ones who dwell in the Garden of Eden, all the trees of the Garden pour out fragrant spices and sing and offer praises. Then he too is aroused and offers praises."

The rooster crows in seven voices:

The first voice says: "Lift up your heads, O you gates; and be lifted up, you everlasting doors; and the King of Glory shall come in. Who is this King of Glory? The Lord strong and mighty, the Lord, mighty in battle." (Ps. 24:7)

The second voice says: "Lift up your heads, O you gates; and lift them up, you everlasting doors, that the King of Glory may come in. Who is this King of Glory? The Lord of Hosts, He is the King of Glory. Selah." (Ps. 24:9)

The third voice says: "Arise, you righteous ones, and busy yourselves with Torah so that your reward will be doubled in the world to come."

The fourth voice says: "I wait for your salvation, O God." (Gen. 49:18)

The fifth voice says: "How long will you sleep, O lazy one?" (Prov. 6:9)

The sixth voice says: "Do not love sleep lest you come to poverty; open your eyes and you shall be satisfied with bread." (Prov. 20:13)

The seventh voice says: "It is time to act for the Lord: they have violated your Torah." (Ps. 119:126)

The chicken says: "He gives food to all flesh. His steadfast love endures forever." (Ps. 136:25)

The dove says: "I piped like a swift or a crane, I moaned like a dove. As my eyes all worn, looked to heaven: 'My Lord, I am in straits; by my surety.'" (Isa. 38:14) The dove speaks before the Holy Blessed One, "Sovereign of the Universe, may my food be as bitter as the olive but entrusted to Your hand rather than sweet as honey and dependent on one of flesh and blood." (Talmud Eruvin 186)

The eagle says: "You, O Lord God of Hosts, God of Israel, bestir yourself to bring all nations to account; have no pity on all the treacherous villains." (Ps. 59:6)

The crane says: "Praise the Lord with the lyre; with the ten-stringed harp sing to Him." (Ps. 33:2)

The sparrow says: "Even the sparrow has

found a home, and the swallow a nest for herself in which to set her young, near your altar, O Lord of Hosts, my King and My God." (Ps. 84:4)

The swallow says: "That my whole being might sing hymns to You unceasingly; O Lord, my God, I will praise You forever." (Ps. 30:13)

The peacock says: "My help is from the Lord who made heaven and earth." (Ps. 121:2)

The desert bird says: "Light is sown for the righteous and gladness for the upright in heart." (Ps. 97:11)

The dove says: "Comfort O comfort, my people, says your God." (Isa. 40:1)

The stork says: "Speak tenderly to Jerusalem, and declare to her that her term of service is over, that her iniquity is expiated; for she has received at the hand of the Lord double for her sins." (Isa. 40:2)

The raven says: "Who provides for the raven his provision when his young ones cry to God?" (Job 38:41)

The starling says: "Their offspring shall be known among the nations, their descendants in the midst of the peoples. All who see them shall recognize that they are a stock the Lord has blessed." (Isa. 61:9) "Sing forth, O righteous, to the Lord; it is fitting that the upright acclaim Him." (Ps. 33:1)

The domestic goose says: "Praise the Lord; call on His Name; proclaim His deeds among the nations. Sing praises to Him; speak of all His wondrous acts." (Ps. 105:1–2)

The goose who lives in the desert, when he sees Israel engaged with Torah, says: "A voice rings out: 'Clear in the desert a road for God. Level in the wilderness a highway for our God.'" (Isa. 40:3) And when finding its food in the desert, the goose says, "Cursed is he who trusts in man." (Jer. 17:5) "Blessed is he who trusts in the Lord, whose trust is in the Lord alone." (Jer. 17:7)

The chicken says: "Trust in the Lord forever, for the Lord God is an everlasting rock." (Isa. 26:4)

The vulture says: "I will whistle to them and gather them, for I will redeem them; they shall increase and continue increasing." (Zech. 10:8)

The butterfly says: "I will lift up my eyes to the mountains, for where does my help come?" (Ps. 121:1)

The locust says: "O Lord you are my God; I will extol you, I will praise your name; for you have done wonderful things, counsels of steadfast faithfulness." (Isa. 25:1)

The spider says, "Praise Him with resounding cymbals, praise him with clanging cymbals." (Ps. 150:5)

The fly, when Israel is not engaged with Torah, says: "A voice rings out: 'Proclaim.' Another asks: 'What shall I proclaim? All flesh is grass, all its goodness like the flower of the field.'" (Is. 40:6) "'Grass withers, flowers fade, but the word of our God shall endure forever.'" (Isa. 40:8) "I will create a new expression of the lips; peace, peace for the far and near says God, and I will heal them." (Isa. 57:19)

The sea monsters say: "Praise the Lord, O you who are on earth, all sea monsters and ocean depths." (Ps. 148:7)

Leviathan says: "Praise God, for He is good, His steadfast love is eternal." (Ps. 136:1)

The fish say: "The voice of God is on the waters, the God of glory thunders, the Lord is upon the mighty waters." (Ps. 29:3)

The frog says: "Blessed be the name of God's glorious majesty forever and ever."

The small cow who is ritually pure says: "Who is like You, O God, among the gods? Who is like You, glorious in holiness, fearful in praises, doing wonders?" (Exod. 15:11)

The large cow who is ritually pure says, "Sing joyously to God, our strength; raise a shout for the God of Jacob." (Ps. 81:2)

The camel says: "God roars from on high, He makes His voice heard from His holy dwelling. God roars aloud over His earthly abode." (Jer. 25:30)

The horse says: "As the eyes of slaves follow their master's hands, as the eyes of a slave girl follow the hand of her mistress, so our eyes are toward the Lord, our God, awaiting God's favor." (Ps. 123:2)

The mule says: "All the kings of the earth shall praise you, O God, for they have heard the words that You spoke." (Ps. 138:4)

The donkey says: "Yours, O God, is the greatness and the power and the glory and the victory and the majesty; for all that is in heaven and on earth is Yours, O God. Yours is the kingdom and you are exalted as head above all." (1 Chron. 29:11)

The bull says: "Then Moses and the Israelites sang this song to God. They said: 'I will sing to God, for He has triumphed gloriously, horse and driver has God hurled into the sea.'" (Exod. 15:1)

The animals of the field say: "Blessed be God who is good and does good."

The deer says: "And I will sing of your strength, extol each morning Your faithfulness. For You have been my haven, a refuge in time of distress." (Ps. 59:17)

The elephant says: "How great are Your works, O God, how very deep are Your thoughts." (Ps. 92:6)

The lion says: "God goes forth like a warrior, like a fighter He whips up His rage. God yells, God roars aloud, God charges upon His enemies." (Isa. 42:13)

The bear says: "Let the desert and its towns cry aloud, the villages where Kedar dwells. Let Sela's inhabitants shout, call out from the peaks of the mountains. Let them do honor to God, and tell His glory in the coastlands." (Isa. 42:11–12)

The wolf says: "In all charges of misappropriation, pertaining to an ox, a donkey, a sheep, a garment, or any other loss, whereof one party alleges, 'This is it'—the case of both parties shall come before God. He whom God declares guilty shall pay double to the other." (Exod. 22:8)

The fox says: "Woe to the one who builds his house by unrighteousness, and his chambers by injustice. Who uses his neighbor's service without pay and does not give him his wages." (Jer. 22:13)

The cat says: "I pursued my enemies and overtook them. I did not turn back till I destroyed them." (Ps. 18:38)

The insects say: "Let Israel rejoice in its Maker, let the children of Zion exult in their King." (Ps. 149:2)

The serpent says: "The Lord supports all who stumble, and makes all who are bent down stand straight." (Ps. 145:14)

The scorpion says: "The Lord is good to all, and His mercy is upon all His works." (Ps. 145:9)

The snail says: "Like a snail that melts away as it moves, like a woman's stillbirth, may they never see the sun." (Ps. 58:9)

The ant says: "Go to the ant, you sluggard. Consider her ways and be wise." (Prov. 6:6)

The mouse says: "And you are righteous about all that befalls us, for you act in truth and we have done evil." (Neh. 9:33)

The rat says: "Let everything that has breath praise God, Hallelujah." (Ps. 150:6)

The dogs say: "Come, let us bow down and

kneel, bend the knee before God our Maker."
(Ps. 95:6)

Blessed be the Lord, God, God of Israel, who
alone does wonders. And blessed be His glorious Name forever. May His glory fill the entire
earth. Amen and Amen.

Fantastic Beasts:
The Jewish
Bestiary

Several fantastic animals inhabit the world of myth and imagination in Jewish legend and folklore. Although you will not find any of these animals in a zoo, these legendary monster-creatures continue to "pop up" in Jewish lore and story. Following is a Who's Who of these legendary monsters.

Behemoth: (plural of *Behemah*—'beast'). Behemoth (Job 40:15–24) was a land monster, sometimes considered to be a mate of the sea monster Leviathan. It is depicted as an animal that eats grass like an ox, is all muscles and strength, lives in the marsh in the shade, eats massive quantities of food, and can swallow the waters of the Jordan. In the light of the description of the other animals in these chapters, it would seem that the reference is to an existing animal, to which legendary details were later added.

According to the Book of Psalms (50:10), Behemoth was created out of 1,000 mountains, and was deprived of the power of procreation so he would not be able to overpopulate the earth.

The hippopotamus has often been identified as Behemoth because it is the largest land animal in the Middle East, weighing up to 6,000 pounds. Like the hippopotamus, Behemoth is a vegetarian. Although in a few legends it does eat animals, Job describes animals playing unconcernedly near it. Most stories agree with Job, saying that Behemoth sheltered birds and that annually at the summer solstice it reared up on its hind legs to roar a warning to wild beasts that they should not attack domestic livestock. Most of Behemoth's time was spent nibbling lotus leaves and reeds along the Nile River.

Apparently what made Behemoth a monster was its amazing size and strength. Job said it had a tail like a cedar and bones as strong as brass.

In later Jewish literature, Behemoth appears as a purely mythical creature. Legend has it that at the end of the world's existence Behemoth will be killed and served along with his mate Leviathan at a banquet tendered for the righteous.

Barnacle-goose: This is a bird that grows on trees, affixed by its bill. Literary interest in this creature continues to exist, partly because it appears in such sources as Aristotle and Shakespeare. Much debate continues to exist as to whether this creature is kosher—by some authorities it is permitted as a fruit and by other it is banned as a shellfish.

Dragon: The dragon was viewed as a gigantic winged crocodile. In the New Testament it is often identified with Satan, idolatry, and sin.

As a creature of the sea, it appears in several places in the Book of Psalms: "You break the heads of dragons in the waters" (Ps. 74:13) and "Praise God from earth, you dragons and all deeps" (Ps. 148:7).

Leviathan: Leviathan was an immense and terrifying sea creature. Biblical scholars who have analyzed Hebrew myths have often identified Leviathan with the primeval sea monster Tiamat, known in the Babylonian creation stories. The characteristics of this monster indicate that it is related to many sea monsters that appear in the Bible. Isaiah (51:9) mentions Rahab, a huge sea dragon that God destroyed while creating the world.

Of all the sea monsters, the one mentioned most often and described in the most graphic detail is Leviathan. The likely reason is the influence of the Canaanite monster Lotan on the myths of the early Hebrews. Lotan in Canaanite texts is described as "a tortuous serpent" with seven heads. In some stories Leviathan also has several heads (Ps. 74:14).

In the stories about both Lotan and Leviathan it takes a deity to destroy the monster. In the case of Lotan, it is Baal, one of the chief Canaanite gods, who crushes the animal. In the Book of Isaiah, God is the one who kills Leviathan (27:1).

The Bible's most detailed description of Leviathan is in Job (41). Light shines from the monster's eyes, sparks and flames shoot from his mouth, and smoke pours from his nostrils as out of a seething caldron. His breath kindles coals and his heart is as firm as stone. Job notes that no person is so bold as to go fishing for Leviathan with a hook or to play with him as with a bird. He is king over all the children of pride and the symbol of evil.

Despite all of the fear of Job's Leviathan, the sea monster appears friendlier in but one place. Psalms (104:26) says that the monster plays in the sea.

Rabbi Yochanan, the source for many of the legends related to Leviathan, describes an elaborate banquet at which time the flesh of Leviathan will be served as a feast for the righteous, particularly pious people who refrain from attending or participating in pagan sporting events (Baba Batra 74a–b). One source attributes Leviathan's death to lethal combat with a second gargantuan beast, Behemoth, while another traces the animal's demise to the hand of God Himself (Lev. Rabbah 13:3). In any event, Leviathan's flesh will comprise the menu for a scrumptious messianic feast.

Phoenix: The Phoenix is a fabulous bird that is mentioned in apocalyptic literature. It has been said that "its food is the manna of heaven and dew of the earth, and from its excrement the cinnamon tree grows" (3 Bar. 6:13). Some commentators contend that the *chol* mentioned in Job 29:18 is the phoenix.

Jewish legend states that this bird lives for a thousand years. At the end of 1,000 years, fire comes out of its nest and consumes it, and leaving behind of itself about the size of an egg, it reproduces limbs and lives again. Another view holds that after a thousand years "its body is consumed, its wings moult" and it renews itself (Gen. Rabbah 19:5).

Re'em: This creature is a giant animal whose entire population consists of only one male and one female. Each lives at the opposite end of the earth from the other, and at the end of 70 years, they find their way to one another to mate. The male dies from a bite inflicted by the female during copulation and the female undergoes a pregnancy of 12 years. Eventually her belly bursts open and out come twins, one male and one female, who depart to opposite ends of the earth. The process begins anew.

Shamir: The shamir is a worm that was created on the twilight before the first Sabbath. Known for its amazing strength, it has the ability to penetrate the hardest diamonds or other precious stones without leaving a grain of dust. According to legend, it could engrave the metal for the breast plate of the *Kohen Gadol*, and because metal tools were not allowed to be used for the building of the Temple, the shamir was used to hew the Temple stones.

Unicorn: The chief characteristics of the biblical unicorn are its strength and its inability to be tamed. The Book of Job (39:9–12) has the longest and most graphic description of the unicorn: "Would the unicorn agree to serve you? Would he spend the night at your crib? Can you hold the unicorn by ropes to the furrow? Would he plow up the valley behind you? Would you rely on his great strength and leave your toil to him? Would you trust him to bring in the seed and gather it in from your threshing floor?" From these verses we can see that the unicorn was neither an animal that one could trust nor was it able to be trained.

Ziz: This creature was the ruler of all of the birds. It was 500 miles high—with its feet on the ground and its head touching the sky. Its wings were large enough to darken the sky when spread. An egg once dropped by the female Ziz crushed three hundred cedars and flooded sixty cities. The immense wingspan of this fowl was capable of eclipsing the light of the sun (Gen. Rabbah 19:4).

Ziz's eventual fate, like that of Leviathan and Behemoth, is a culinary one. Its flesh will be eaten at a future repast for righteous people as a reward for those who abstained from eating forbidden species of fowl.

In addition to the aforementioned creatures, rabbinic legend also endows several biblical animals with amazing characteristics. Here is an enumeration of these animals with impressive origins:

1. The snake in the Book of Genesis had the ability to talk (Gen. 3).

2. The ram that Abraham sacrificed instead of Isaac was said to have been created on the twilight of the first Sabbath eve. Its ashes were said to comprise the foundation of the future Temple altar while its horn was destined to be

sounded atop Mount Sinai during the revelatory experience (Pirke de Rabbi Eliezer 31).

3. Balaam's donkey was gifted with the power of speech (Num. 22, 23), and according to the Ethics of the Fathers was especially created for its role on the sixth day of creation.

4. Noah's dove was depicted as actually being able to talk to God as she declares: "May my food be as bitter as the olive but entrusted to Your hand rather than be sweet as honey and dependent on a human" (Talmud Eruvin 18b).

5. Jonah was swallowed by a fish large enough to allow him to survive inside for 3 days.

6. A unique one-horned creature known as the *tachash* was brought into existence so that its skin could be used as the material for the tabernacle erected in the wilderness (Talmud Shabbat 28b).

7. The golden calf that was fashioned by the Israelites could actually move about at will, as if alive (Tanchuma Ki Tissa 19:24).

8. King Solomon was transported to distant lands by a giant eagle. He also rode a large sea turtle at his coronation (Eccles. Rabbah 2:25).

9. Sifre Shemini (6) describes a creature called the *adne hasadeh*, a plant-man with leaves sprouting forth from his head.

10. The Tosefot to Bechorot (1:11) describes dolphins that were half human and half fish.

11. The Sifra to Shemini (3) makes reference to the existence of mermaids.

12. The Talmud of Eruvin (18a) describes the first man as sporting the tail of an animal.

Biblical Names Linked to the Animal World

Many human personal names are linked to the world of animals. Following is a listing of some of the names that are connected to various animals.

1. Rachel (meaning a ewe)
2. Hamor (meaning a donkey)
3. Tola (meaning a worm)
4. Tzipporah (meaning a bird)
5. Gazez (meaning one who shears sheep)
6. Shual (meaning a fox)
7. Eglon (meaning a calf)
8. Ya'el (meaning a mountain goat)
9. Orev (meaning a raven)
10. Zibia (meaning a gazelle)
11. Jonah (meaning a dove)
12. Aryeh (meaning a lion)
13. Z'ev (meaning a wolf)
14. Dov (meaning a bear)
15. Deborah (meaning a bee)

16. Chayah (meaning a living being)
17. Ayalah (meaning a hind)
18. Tzvee (meaning a deer)
19. Ari (meaning a lion)

The Jewish Dietary Laws: "Clean" and "Unclean" Animals

The first biblical person to be permitted to eat meat was Noah: "Every moving thing that lives shall be for you" (Gen. 9:3). Adam, the first human being created by God, was forbidden to eat meat. Just as at the beginning of time in the perfect society symbolized by the Garden of Eden, there was no eating of meat, so at the end of time, in the messianic era as described by the prophet Isaiah, there will be a return to the original state: "And the wolf shall dwell with the lamb, and the leopard shall lie down with the kid . . . and the lion shall eat straw like the ox . . . they shall not hurt nor destroy in all My holy mountain" (Isa. 11:6). Here the inference is generally drawn that if the carnivorous animal will disappear at the end of time, how much more so the carnivorous human being.

Human consumption of meat, which means of course the taking of an animal life, has constantly posed a religious problem in Judaism, even when it accepted the necessity of it. The Talmudic rabbis were always aware of the distinction between man's ideal and his real condition regarding food. Referring to Deuteronomy (12:20), they said that "the Torah teaches a lesson in moral conduct, that man shall not eat meat unless he has a special craving for it, and shall eat it only occasionally and sparingly" (Talmud Chullin 84a).

The permission to eat meat in Judaism has often been described as a compromise, a divine concession, so-to-speak, to human weakness and human need. The Bible forbade the eating of blood with the animals, because "blood is the life, and you shall not eat the life with the flesh" (Deut. 12:23). From this verse we see the Bible's emphasis on the reverence for life that it so desires humans to have, and thus the prohibition of eating blood.

Most of the prohibitions regarding forbidden foods are listed in Leviticus (11) and Deuteronomy (14:3–20). Animals that did not have split hooves or did not chew their cuds were forbidden. Aquatic animals that lack fins and scales, such as the eel, are forbidden. Birds of prey and carrion eaters were forbidden. Animals that died of themselves or were killed by another animal were forbidden. Fat that was attached to an animal's stomach, extending over the intestines, was forbidden. In quadrupeds, the sciatic sinew had to be removed from the slaughtered animal before it could be eaten. Small creeping things and winged insects were forbidden. The above two biblical passages enumerating permissible and forbidden animals are almost identical in their language as well as substance. Three times the Bible repeated the command: "You shall not boil a kid in its mother's milk" (Exod. 23:1, 34:26; Deut. 14:21). According to some, this was part of a Canaanite ritual, and hence prohibited as a pagan custom. This prohibition may also have been intended to preserve the natural instincts of humanity that distinguished the Israelites from the barbarous nations that surrounded them.

The Bible also states that the people of Israel are sanctified by eating the so-called "unclean" or prohibited foods. But it does not explain why those foods have a defiling effect.

RATIONALES FOR
JEWISH DIETARY LAWS

Many theories have been proposed to explain the rationale of the dietary laws, ranging from hygienic reasons, to moralistic or nationalistic. Here is a summary of these rationales, culled from both traditional as well as modern sources.

Philo: This ancient philosopher states that the dietary laws are intended to teach the Jewish people control of their bodily appetites. He further finds a symbolic meaning in the permission to eat animals that chew their cud and have divided hoofs. He says that a person grows in wisdom only if he repeats and chews over what he has studied and if he learns to divide and distinguish various concepts.

Maimonides: This medieval philosopher states that the purpose of keeping the Jewish dietary laws is to inculcate self-control, but to this he also adds that these regulations are also health laws. Many of the forbidden animals are injurious to human health, and in addition are also aesthetically repulsive (e.g., eels and roaches).

Nachmonides: This commentator, with regard to the prohibition of eating fish that do not have fins and scales, says that fish with fins and scales swim close to the water surface, where they frequently come up for air. This warms their blood, and unlike fish that do not have fins and scales, allows them to rid themselves of various impurities.

Joseph Hertz: This former chief rabbi of Great Britain suggests that outward consecration of certain foods symbolically expressed an inner sanctity. By keeping the Jewish dietary laws, the people of Israel would always remind themselves of their status as a holy people, separate from the other nations of the world.

Mary Douglas: This anthropologist suggests that holiness means keeping distinct categories of creation. She believed, therefore, that the biblical categories would classify as unacceptable or unclean any foods from species that are imperfect members of their class, or whose class itself confounds the general scheme of the world. The dietary laws, are, therefore, signs that inspire meditation on the oneness, purity, and completeness of God. By following rules of avoidance, holiness is given a physical expression in every human encounter with the animal kingdom and at every meal.

Sforno: This commentator states that the significance of the prohibition of eating the thigh muscle is to symbolically demonstrate that a Jew must never allow a physical handicap to discourage him in his fight for survival.

Hinnuch: He states that the reason for not eating animals that had been killed by a beast of prey relate to health. He states that such animals are unhealthy and therefore not to be eaten.

Ibn Ezra: He states that the ancient practice of cooking a kid in its mother's milk was a form of barbarism and cruelty to animals, and that is why it was forbidden. He further states that insects were forbidden because it is impossible for a person who ate these to have a pure, clean, and holy conscience.

Nachmonides: He states that the reason for the prohibition of eating blood was to prevent our bodies from absorbing animalistic characteristics. If humans refrain from eating blood, which is the source of life and the very soul of the animal, they will be less likely to take on the animal's vitality or instincts. With regard to the prohibition of eating fish that do not have fins or scales, he asserts that such fish are stationary and are more like earthbound creatures. Thus, they are out of their element in the water and therefore forbidden to be eaten.

A PARTIAL LISTING OF PROHIBITED AND PERMITTED FOODS

Kosher refers to foods that are fit to be eaten. *Terefah* refers to foods that are not fit for consumption. Permitted animals must chew their cud and have split hooves. (The meat must also be killed according to the traditional Jewish laws of slaughtering.) The method consists of cutting the throat with a single, swift, and uninterrupted horizontal sweep of the knife in such a way as to sever the trachea, esophagus, carotid arteries, and jugular vein. The knife blade must be perfect—sharper and smoother than a surgeon's scalpel and free from nicks.

With regard to fish, all of those having fins and scales are kosher and therefore permissible to be eaten. Permissible fowl according to the rabbinical law possess the following characteristics: they are not birds of prey, one toe must be larger than the others, the birds must have a crop, and they must have a gizzard of which the inner lining can be easily removed.

Finally, with regard to insects, locusts are permitted according to the Bible if they have four wings that cover most of the length and breadth of their bodies, four feet, and jointed legs. All other "creeping things" are forbidden. The product of an insect that is not a part of its body is permitted to be eaten (e.g., honey from bees).

Because of the laws of kosher slaughter, Jews are forbidden to kill animals through hunting. This method of slaughter automatically renders an animal unkosher. This prohibition seems to have been incorporated into the Jewish psyche, and as a whole Jewish people do not hunt animals for sport.

Kosher slaughtering is designed to cause the animal the least possible amount of pain. With regard to the slaughter of an animal according to traditional Jewish law, as soon as the animal is killed by a slaughterer trained in Jewish custom who is pious and observant (called a *shochet* in Hebrew), the animal is positioned so as to allow its blood to drain. Since some blood remains, the meat is purged to remove all residual blood. The butcher removes veins, sacs, and the various membranes that collect blood, and then either the butcher or the traditional Jewish homemaker soaks, salts, and rinses the meat to further extract the remaining blood.

As a rule, permitted animals are herbivorous. Permitted animals (if slaughtered according to traditional Jewish law) would include:

cow
deer
goat
lamb
sheep

Forbidden ones would include:

bison
horse
pig
rabbit

Permitted fowl include:

capon
chicken
dove
duck
goose
pigeon
turkey

Forbidden fowl include:

bat
cuckoo
eagle
hawk

heron
kite
lapwing
ostrich
owl
pelican
stork
swan
vulture

Permitted fish include:

anchovy
bluefish
butterfish
carp
cod
flounder
fluke
haddock
halibut
herring
mackerel
pike
porgy
red snapper
salmon
sardine
seabass

shad
smelt
sole
trout
tuna
weakfish
whitefish

Forbidden fish and aquatic animals include:

bullfish
catfish
clam
crab
eel
frog
lobster
monkfish
octopus
oyster
scallop
shark
shrimp
snail
wolfish

Animals in Selected Short Stories

THE GOATS THAT ONCE
WERE CHICKENS*

One hot afternoon, Jacob walked home carrying a sackful of chickens he had bought at the marketplace. He was tired, and when he saw the shady doorway of a house, he stopped to rest. Carefully he placed the chickens on the ground beside him, leaned back, and fell asleep.

"Sleeping, Jacob?" His friend Avram woke him up. "Come. Miriam sent me to look for you. Don't you know how late it is?"

Jacob was so flustered by his friend's message that he jumped up and went with Avram, leaving his chickens behind.

Cackle. Cackle. Cackle. The chickens' noises grew louder and louder as they squirmed in their sack, trying to free themselves.

Rabbi Hanina ben Dosa, who lived in the

---

*Goldin, Barbara, *A Child's Book of Midrash* (Northvale, NJ: Jason Aronson Inc. 1990) pp. 51–53.

house, heard the noise. "Those chickens sound like they're in our yard," he said.

"I'll go see," said his wife.

When she stepped outside, she saw the wiggling sack tied with green rope near the doorway.

"What shall I do with this?" she asked her husband, showing him the sack.

"Probably the owner forgot them," Rabbi Hanina said. "We'll care for his chickens until he comes."

Rabbi Hanina's wife fed the chickens and gave them water. They ran around in the yard, and in and out of the house.

One day went by. Two. Three. More. Still the owner did not come for his chickens.

The hens began to lay eggs. The Rabbi's wife brought the first one to show her husband.

"Look, we have eggs now," she told him.

"We mustn't eat any of the eggs," Rabbi Hanina said. "They belong to the owner. He'll come back for them."

Even though the Rabbi and his wife were very poor and sometimes hungry, they left the eggs alone. The hens sat on their eggs and before long, the eggs hatched into active little chicks.

Hen, roosters, and chicks filled the yard and the house, scrambling under tables and chairs while Rabbi Hanina studied and his wife cooked and baked. Cackle, cackle. Cock-a-doodle. Cheep, cheep. Sounds also filled the yard and the house.

Two months went by. Three. Four. More. Still the owner did not come for his chickens.

"We must do something," said the Rabbi's wife, as she scattered the last of the chickens' grain around the yard.

"Yes, we must," agreed the Rabbi, who had to study with his fingers stuffed in his ears. "I know. I'll sell the chickens and buy goats. We won't have to feed the goats. They can graze on the forest floor."

One year went by. Two. Three. More.

Then one day, Jacob was walking near Rabbi Hanina's house with Avram when he stopped.

"Avram," he said. "Remember that time I forgot my chickens? I went looking for them, but couldn't find the right house or the sack?"

"I remember."

"This house reminds me of the one I stopped at to rest."

Rabbi Hanina, who had been standing by the open window and heard Jacob, came running out of his house.

"Friend. Stop a minute. What kind of sack did you say you left?"

Jacob straightened suddenly, startled by the Rabbi.

"Why, years ago I left a large sack of chickens tied with green rope near here."

"Then I have something to show you." Rabbi Hanina led Jacob and Avram to the goat shed. "Here are your chickens. You may take them with you."

"But these are goats!" Jacob looked very confused.

Rabbi Hanina laughed.

"Your chicken family grew so large that I sold them and bought goats."

"Rabbi Hanina, you are so kind. I've never met anyone so careful to return lost things," said Jacob. He tied up the goats and led them out of the yard with Avram.

Jacob smiled and waved.

Rabbi Hanina ran inside to tell his wife.

"The owner came for his chickens," he called.

"At last. It was a good thing we kept them for him all these years," said his wife. "But tell me, did he recognize them?"

THE PIOUS COW*

Eliezer's cow was strong and healthy and a very good worker. Every day she pulled his plow through the fields—every day except the Sabbath. For Eliezer was Jewish and rested on the seventh day. His animals rested too.

Eliezer and his cow worked hard together for many years. But after several meager harvests, Eliezer became poor and was forced to sell his possessions, including his beloved cow.

During the first few days, the cow worked hard for her new master, just as she had for Eliezer. But her new owner did not observe the Jewish customs and when it came to the seventh day, he did not rest as Eliezer had. He worked every day, one day being just like another.

When the Sabbath came, the new owner tried to hitch the cow to his plough, but she would not budge. He yelled commands to her. "Go! Forward! Go!" Still she would not budge. Then he beat her angrily with his whip. The cow did not move.

The new owner ran to Eliezer's house. "What

---

*Goldin, pp. 89–90.

kind of a cow did you sell me? She won't work. She won't even get up. I want all my money back. Every bit of it."

"I don't understand," said Eliezer. "She was always such a good worker. Wait. Did she work yesterday?"

"Yes, she did," admitted the new owner.

"And the day before?" Eliezer asked.

"Yes. But she won't even get up today."

"Take me to her," said Eliezer.

The two men walked over to the field where the cow lay resting, chewing some grass.

"See what I mean?" said the new owner, pointing to the cow. "Now does she look like a good worker to you?"

Eliezer bent down and whispered something into the cow's ear.

Soon the cow was up, ready to work. Her new owner could not believe the change.

"What did you say to her?" he asked.

"I told her that when she belonged to me, we all rested on the Sabbath, as God commanded. But now she belongs to a new master who isn't Jewish, and who does not rest on the Sabbath. So she must work also, as does her master."

The new owner grew thoughtful. "This animal has learned to keep the rest day while I, a human, work seven days with no rest and no knowledge of my Creator. I believe I will follow your cow's lead," he said to Eliezer.

He took the cow back to the barn and did no more work that day or on the other Sabbath days to come. Soon he began to study the Jewish laws and not only became a Jew, but a rabbi as well. He was known as Rabbi Hanina ben Torta, Rabbi Hanina, son of the cow.

THE ROOSTER
WHO WOULD BE KING*

A long time ago, there lived a King and Queen and their son the Prince. They considered this prince to be their jewel, their greatest treasure—the apple of their eye. The King made certain that the Prince had the most learned teachers and the wisest soothsayers to instruct him in all that a prince would need to know in order to be a great king, when the time came for him to rule the kingdom.

One day, a strange illness overcame the Prince, and he began to act like a rooster. He took off his clothes and roamed all around the palace, flapping his arms like a rooster and crowing loud and long. He also stopped speaking the language of the King and Queen. He ate only corn from the floor, like a rooster, and refused to sit at the table with others, eating only *under* the table *alone*.

The King and Queen became very upset and called for the best doctors in the kingdom to treat the Prince, in hopes of curing him of his

---

*Schram, Peninnah, *Jewish Stories One Generation Tells Another* (Northvale, NJ: Jason Aronson Inc. 1987) pp. 293–95.

illness. But nothing that the doctors and the soothsayers and the other healers tried seemed to make any difference and the Rooster Prince continued happily crowing and flapping his arms, and hopping around in the palace, wherever he wanted to go.

One day, a wise old man came to the palace. "Your Majesty, I would like to try to cure the Prince," he said to the King.

"Where are your medicines?" asked the surprised King, because all the doctors carried at least one bag filled with bottles of potions and oils.

"I have my own ways, Your Majesty," answered the wise man. "Allow me seven days *alone* with the Prince."

The King reluctantly agreed, since there was no other hope.

The wise man was brought to the Prince. The first thing he did was to take off all of *his* clothing, jump under the table, and sit opposite the Rooster Prince. The Prince stared at the stranger for a very long time.

"Who are you, and what are you doing here?" crowed the Rooster Prince curiously.

"I am a rooster. Can't you see that?" answered the wise man matter-of-factly but patiently.

"Oh, I am a rooster, too. Welcome!" replied the Prince, happy to have found a friend.

Time passed with the two companions crowing and flapping their arms.

One day, the stranger got out from under the table and began to walk around—a little straighter each day. The Rooster Prince had grown so fond of his friend that he began to follow him wherever he went. And the two roosters hopped around the palace together.

On another day, the wise man put on a shirt and a pair of trousers. "What are you wearing, my friend?" asked the Rooster Prince. "Roosters don't wear clothes!"

"You're right, dear Prince, but I was a bit chilled. However, I assure you, you can still be a good rooster even with clothes on. Try it," challenged the wise man.

The Rooster Prince put some clothes on, too—and continued crowing and flapping his arms.

The next day, the wise man sat at the table and ate some corn from a golden platter. The Rooster Prince sat next to his friend. The wise man signaled to the servants and soon the table was set with silverware, goblets, and golden plates. Slowly, the wise man began to eat all the delicious food—in a proper manner—and the Prince began to imitate him.

Soon a whole meal was eaten, and the Rooster Prince crowed most happily.

The following night, the wise man began to sleep on a bed. He again assured the Prince. "Don't worry, my Prince, you can be a good rooster just the same, even sleeping on a bed." And so the Rooster Prince resumed sleeping on his royal bed and no longer slept under the table.

Soon after, the wise man began to discuss the philosophy of life with the Prince. "Wait a minute, roosters don't have to think, and they certainly don't debate the merits of a way of life," declared the Prince. "Roosters just exist, being fed and cared for without any worries."

"You may be right," answered his wise old friend, "but on the other hand, it doesn't mean you can't be a good rooster if you do engage in discussion. After all, *you* will know that you are a rooster, just the same."

The Prince thought this over, and began to discuss philosophical ideas with the wise man.

On the seventh day, the wise man bid farewell to the Prince. As he was about to leave, he said, "My friend, remember—roosters are fair game for the hunter. So always try to pretend you are a human prince. Act wisely and help others. Farewell!"

From that day on, the Prince walked, ate, and talked like the prince he was.

And when, in time, he became a great King ruling over that entire kingdom, no one besides himself knew that he was still a rooster.

LEVIATHAN*

On the fifth day of creation God also made Leviathan. Just as Ziz-Shaddai is the King of the Birds, so Leviathan is the King of the Sea. At first there were two such creatures in the sea, but so terrible was their power, so insatiable their thirst, that God destroyed the female, leaving the male to rule alone. Yet even this single sea monster threatens to overwhelm the earth, for each day Leviathan gulps down all the water from the Jordan River as it flows into the sea. And when he's hungry, his hot breath boils the seas until they seethe like a stewpot.

How strangely is this creature made! His gigantic fins blaze with lightning, outshining the sun. His flashing eyes light up the entire sea. Every day God leaves heaven to play with Leviathan in the waves.

But oh—the beast's terrible smell! So repulsive is the odor of his breath that it would kill all living things on earth were it not for the fact that each morning Leviathan thrusts his great

---

*Frankel, Ellen, *The Classic Tales* (Northvale, NJ: Jason Aronson Inc. 1989) pp. 10–11.

pointed snout into Paradise to perfume himself with the heavenly fragrance.

At the End of Days the righteous will feast on Leviathan along with Ziz-Shaddai and the mighty Behemoth. Leviathan's wife, killed by God at the beginning of creation, is already prepared for the messianic table, pickled in brine.

And how will the angels slay this mighty sea dragon? They will not be able to, for his steely scales will turn back their swords and spears. No, God will have to send Behemoth, the King of Land Beasts, to combat him. They will slash each other to death with their fierce tails. The beasts' flesh will then feed the pious at the final feast of souls. From the shining skin of Leviathan, God will fashion tents to shelter the righteous, and what remains of the skin will be stretched over Jerusalem, its radiant light illuminating the entire world.

ZIZ-SHADDAI*

On the fifth day, God created the birds. The king of the birds is Ziz-Shaddai, whose feet rest upon the earth and whose head brushes the top of the sky. When he flies across the sun, his enormous wings turn day into night.

And what a wonderful taste the flesh of this bird has! So varied is its flavor that it tastes different to each person who eats it, both like this—*zeh*—and like that—*va-zeh*. Hence its name: Ziz. At the End of Days all the righteous will gather at the messianic banquet to feast upon this wondrous dish. And the heavenly waiter will be Moses himself!

Many legends have arisen about this wonderful bird. Once a ship passed by where Ziz was wading, and the passengers saw that the water only lapped at the creature's ankles.

"Surely this is a fine place to bathe," they said, "for the water is not too deep." And they readied themselves to jump in.

Then a heavenly voice thundered out of the sky, saying, "Do you wish to drown yourselves? Once a carpenter dropped his ax just at this

---

*Frankel, pp. 9–10.

spot, and it took seven years for it to reach the bottom."

Then they knew that the bird they had spied was none other than Ziz-Shaddai.

Another time an egg from Ziz-Shaddai's nest accidentally rolled down a mountainside and cracked. The impact felled sixty giant cedars in the forest of Lebanon. The fluid from the cracked egg flooded sixty cities.

But such misfortunes are rare, for God appointed Ziz-Shaddai to guard the earth from the harsh winds of storm and winter chill. Its wings spread from one end of the earth to the other, sheltering us all like God's own canopy of peace.

THE RE'EM*

On the sixth day of creation God fashioned the beasts of the earth. One of the most wondrous of these beasts was the Re'em.

God made only two of these creatures at the beginning, and no more than two are alive at any one time. For there is not enough food and water on the whole earth to feed more than two of these monstrous beasts. They divide the world between them, the male always dwelling in the east and the female in the west.

Once in seventy years they come together to mate. As soon as the male joins with the female, she turns round her head and bites him so that he dies. Then she remains pregnant for twelve years. For the first eleven years, she moves about and grazes. But in the twelfth year, her belly grows so heavy that she can no longer stand, and she falls down upon her side. There she lies for the next twelve months, spittle drooling from her mouth and watering the grass beside her so that she can feed herself and her growing young.

At the end of the twelfth year, her womb

---

*Frankel, pp. 14–15.

splits open and twin calves emerge, one female and one male. At that instant, the mother dies and the two young depart, one for the east and one for the west. For the next seventy years, they remain apart until, like their parents before them, they meet again to mate and die.

At the time of the Flood, when Noah was commanded to take all the animals into the ark, only the pregnant Re'em was too large to fit inside, so he tied her to the back of the ark and she ran behind, her horned head just reaching above the crest of the floodwaters.

Very few people have encountered this marvelous creature and lived to tell the tale. One such brave soul was King David, when he was still only a shepherd boy tending his father's flocks. One day he chanced upon the Re'em asleep and mistook it for a mountain. Up he climbed until he was perched upon the giant beast's back. Suddenly the Re'em awoke and David found himself high up in the air, caught between the beast's sharp horns. At that moment David vowed that if he were to escape harm this day, he would one day build a temple to God as high as the Re'em's horns, which was very high indeed.

And God heard David's promise and immediately sent a lion to that very spot, which frightened even the mighty Re'em to its knees. As the giant creature bowed its horny head low, David quickly jumped to the ground. And before the lion had a chance to notice the helpless young boy, God sent a deer running by, which the lion chased into the forest.

And so the future king of Israel escaped both monsters without so much as a scratch. And in time, his son Solomon fulfilled his vow.

LEVIATHAN AND THE FOX*

How hard God worked in creating a new world, filled with so many wonderful creatures! When all was finished, it was at last time to rest. But along came the Angel of Death to disturb God's first *Shabbat*. Seeing all the new creatures in God's world, the Angel declared, "Master of the Universe, You fashioned me to be the lord of death. Now give me power over all Your creatures."

"Take a pair of all living things," answered God, "and hurl them into the sea. Then you shall have power over all the rest of their kind."

And that is precisely what the Angel of Death did.

But Fox was too wise for him. When he saw the Angel coming, he began to weep and wail so loudly that the Angel stared at him in amazement.

"Why do you cry so bitterly?" he asked Fox.

"Look in the sea," answered wily Fox. "What do you see?"

The Angel of Death peered down into the

---

*Frankel, pp. 11–14.

water. "Why, I see another Fox!" he cried, for at that moment Fox bent over the water to cast his reflection in the shallows.

"Indeed," wailed Fox, wiping a tear from his long red nose, "two of my friends have fallen into the sea and drowned!" And he lifted up his head and began to cry even more bitterly.

"Then I have no need to drown you," said the Angel.

"What fools you are!" laughed Fox. "Have you ever heard of an animal who travels without his heart?"

"Then you tricked us!" they cried.

"Yes, indeed I have. I fooled the Angel of Death, and now I have fooled Leviathan. They do not call me wise for nothing!"

When the fishes returned to their King and told him what had happened, he said, "Indeed, he is a crafty fellow and you are all fools."

And right then and there, he ate them all up.

THE SHAMIR*

On twilight of the sixth day of creation, God created the Miracles: the pit that swallowed Korakh, the mouth of Miriam's well, Balaam's talking ass, the rainbow, the heavenly manna, Moses' rod, the magically suspended letters of the Ten Commandments, the First Tongs that made all other tongs, and the Shamir.

The Shamir was a marvelous creature, no bigger than a single grain of barley, but so strong that it could cut through any substance on earth, even the hardest diamonds. Only lead alone could contain it.

For safekeeping God gave the Shamir to the Hoopoe-bird, who promised to guard it with her life. With the little worm tight in her beak, the Hoopoe flew throughout the earth, dropping the Shamir upon desolate mountaintops so that the mountaintops split open and blossomed forth into life.

For eons, the Hoopoe kept the Shamir safe in Paradise, departing with it only to seed the mountaintops, until one day God borrowed it back for a special task. It was then that the Israelites were wandering on their forty-year

---

*Frankel, pp. 24–26.

journey in the wilderness. Aaron, the high priest, was ready to take on God's holy work in the Tabernacle, but for this sacred work, he needed a special breastplate made of twelve precious stones, one for each tribe. How could the Israelite artisans engrave the tribes' names on these stones without splintering them? For to etch the words required great strength but also the greatest accuracy and craft. Only the miraculous Shamir was capable of such a task.

So Bezalel and his artisans inscribed the names in ink on each of the stones: ruby, topaz, smaragd, garnet, sapphire, emerald, zircon, agate, amethyst, beryl, jasper, onyx. And then God sent the Shamir to perform its work, etching the names into the shimmering surface of the stones, working with such astonishing skill that not one atom of stone was lost.

Then God returned the Shamir to the Hoopoe's charge.

Where did the Hoopoe keep such a powerful creature? What ordinary vessel could possibly hold it? Since lead alone could resist the Hoopoe's bite, the bird sealed up her precious charge inside a box of lead, wrapped in a woolen cloth nestled among a handful of barley grains.

And there she might have kept it forever had not Solomon needed it to build the Holy Temple in Jerusalem. But that is another story.

For Further Reading
and Exploration

BOOKS

Bodenheimer, F. S. (1960). *Animal and Man in Bible Land*. Leiden.

Cohen, N. (1959). *Tsaar Baale Hayim*. Washington, DC.

Douglas, M. (1976). *Purity and Danger*. New York: Praeger Publishers.

Dresner, S. H., and Siegel, S. (1966). *The Jewish Dietary Laws*. New York: Burning Bush Press.

Feliks, J. (1962). *The Animal World of the Bible*. Tel Aviv.

Fisher, J. (1977). *Scriptural Animals*. New York: Weathervane.

Frankel, E. (1989). *The Classic Tales*. Northvale, NJ: Jason Aronson.

Freedman, S. E. (1970). *The Book of Kashrut*. New York: Bloch.

Goldin, B. D. (1990). *A Child's Book of Midrash*. Northvale, NJ: Jason Aronson.

Hallevi, J. (1946). *Book of Kuzari*. New York: Pardes Publishers.

Maimonides, M. (1963). *The Guide of the Perplexed*. Trans. Shlomo Pines. Chicago: University of Chicago Press.

Schram, P. (1987). *Jewish Stories One Generation Tells Another*. Northvale, NJ: Jason Aronson.

Shochet, E. J. (1984). *Animal Life in Jewish Tradition*. New York: Ktav.

Toperoff, S. P. (1995). *The Animal Kingdom in Jewish Thought*. Northvale, NJ: Jason Aronson.

ORGANIZATIONS

Canadian Wildlife Federation
(society for the protection of wildlife)
1673 Carling Ave.
Ottawa, Ontario, Canada

Hai Bar Society for the Establishment of
    Biblical National Wildlife Preserves
(sets up wildlife sanctuaries)
% Nature Reserves Authority
78 Yirmeyahu St.
Jerusalem, Israel 94467

Jewish Vegetarian Society
210 Riverside Dr.
New York, NY 10025

National Audubon Society
(opposes killing of plumbed birds for use of
    feathers in hats)
700 Broadway
New York, NY 10003

National Wildlife Federation
1400 Sixteenth St., NW
Washington, D.C. 20036

World Wildlife Fund
1250 24th St., NW
Washington, D.C. 20037

Index

About the Author

Rabbi Ronald H. Isaacs has been the spiritual leader of Temple Sholom in Bridgewater, NJ, since 1975. He received his doctorate in instructional technology from Columbia University's Teachers College. He is the author of more than fifty books. His most recent publications include *Every Person's Guide to Death and Dying in the Jewish Tradition* and *Every Person's Guide to Jewish Philosophy and Philosophers*. Rabbi Isaacs currently serves on the publications committee of the Rabbinical Assembly of America and with his wife Leora designs and coordinates the adult learning summer experience called Shabbat Plus at Camp Ramah in the Poconos. He resides in New Jersey with his wife, Leora, and their children, Keren and Zachary.